Bead-opedia

the only beading reference you'll ever need

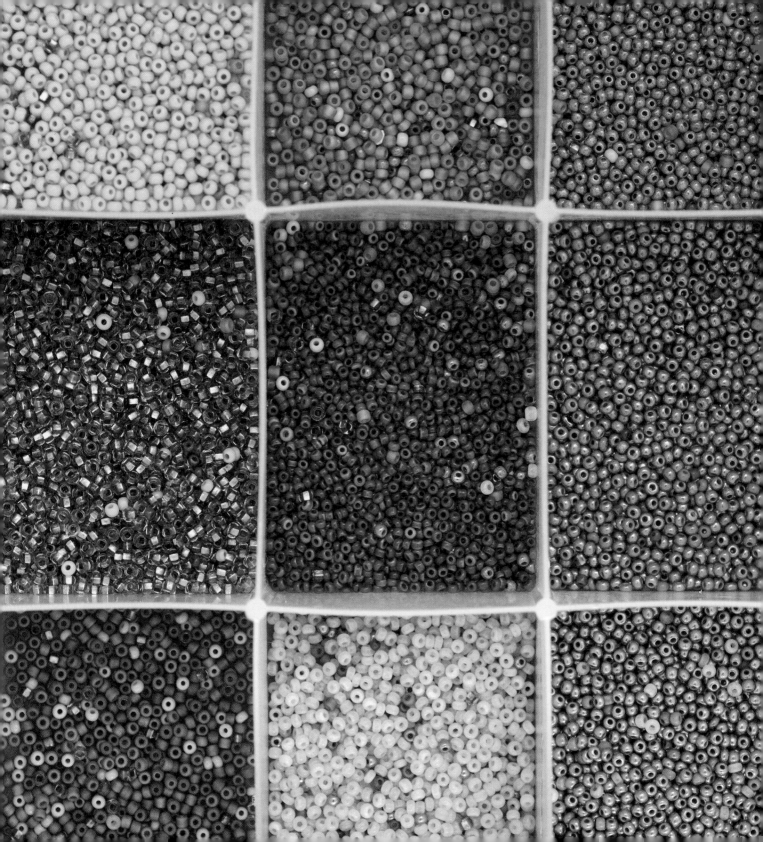

Bead-opedia
The only beading reference you'll ever need

Kerrie Berrie

St. Martin's Griffin
New York

Contents

BEAD-OPEDIA. Copyright © 2015 by Quintet. All rights reserved. Printed in China. For information, address St. Martin's Press, 175 Fifth Avenue, New York, N.Y. 10010.

www.stmartins.com

Library of Congress Cataloging-in-Publication Data Available Upon Request

ISBN 978-1-250-06782-1

St. Martin's Griffin books may be purchased for educational, business, or promotional use. For information on bulk purchases, please contact Macmillan Corporate and Premium Sales Department at 1-800-221-7945, extension 5442, or write to specialmarkets@macmillan.com.

First U.S. Edition: September 2015

QTT.BEDO

Photography: Neil Grundy
Illustrator: Bernard Chau
Designer: Bonnie Bryan
Project Editor: Katy Denny
Art Director: Michael Charles
Editorial Director: Jo Turner
Publisher: Mark Searle

Manufactured in China

10 9 8 7 6 5 4 3 2 1

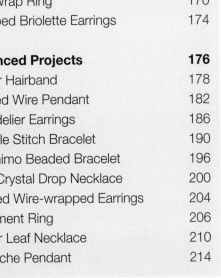

Projects

Introduction

The art of making beaded jewelry and other precious objects has been around for many thousands of years, on every continent and in every major culture.

Earring which shows the Pharaoh in the center of the clip. Part of Tutankhamun's Treasures, gold, 18th Dynasty, c.1340BCE. From the Tomb of Tutankhamun, Thebes.

Early History

There is plenty of archeological evidence to show that prehistoric man used shells, bones, and stones to create beads. The earliest known beads were made from Nassarius sea snail shells and these have been dated as far back as 100,000 years ago.

In ancient Egypt a rough glass substance called faience was used to create small tubular and round beads, often in different colors and patterns, and these were used together with beads made from precious stones and gold to create complex and intricate jewelry.

In ancient China and Japan, jade and bone were carved into exquisitely detailed beads, while porcelain and cinnabar were made as far back as 1300BCE by unknown technologically advanced processes.

Glass beads were being made around 2500BCE, but a little more recently were popularized by the Italian Murano glassmakers from the end of the thirteenth century. Techniques using glass seed beads and wire, such as French beaded flowers, are thought to have been practiced as early as the sixteenth century.

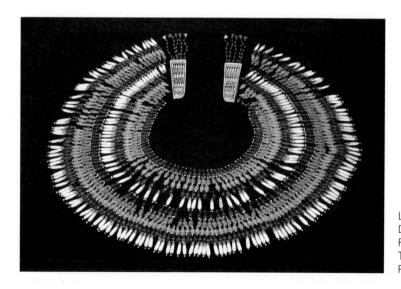

Left; Necklace, 18th Dynasty, circa 1340BCE. From the Tomb of Tutankhamun, Thebes. Right; Murano glass beads.

Storytelling Beads

Beads carved to look like people or animals have been used as a means to tell stories in many cultures. The beads would be strung onto a cord in the correct sequence to relay the events in a story. In some Native American tribes flat beads would be carved with symbols and figures to convey parts of a story.

Not dissimilar to story beads, prayer beads or rosaries are also used to represent a sequence, with each bead representing a prayer. This helps the bearer to remember all the prayers that should be said.

Trading with Beads

European traders began doing business with African countries from the fifteenth century, and beads were a popular form of "currency," earning them the name "trade beads." The African resources that the Europeans sought included materials such as gold and ivory—but also people, and so beads from this era are often called "slave beads."

From the mid-eighteenth century European bead trade houses began to produce bead catalogs of their products, and many survive today in museum collections.

Bead Collecting

Many people enjoy collecting beads from around the world, with the rarest and most sought-after examples fetching prices in the thousands of dollars. In 1992 a single Roman glass bead sold at auction for over $5,000, and necklaces made from jade beads have been known to sell for prices around the $1 million mark. Jade is not only highly prized today—the ancient Mexicans prized jade as a symbol of water and therefore life, and the Mayans are known to have placed jade beads in the mouths of the dead.

Tibetan Dzi beads are passed down through generations, with the methods that were used to create the patterns on the stone beads now lost in the mists of time. The beads hold spiritual meaning and are believed to act as an amulet for the wearer, keeping away evil spirits and neutralizing the "evil eye." It comes as no surprise, then, that these beads are valued and collected not only within Tibet but all around the world.

Modern Jewelry Making

There are now hundreds of different products on the market for making beaded jewelry and the range of techniques involved is vast, making it a very exciting craft to learn—there are almost endless possibilities for the types of jewelry that you can make. However, the mass of choices available can seem a little daunting when you first start out, with such a huge array of beads, findings, tools, and terminology. *Beado-pedia* will simplify all of this, with clear instructions and simple, useful descriptions, forming an invaluable reference as you work through your beading designs.

In the time I've spent developing my own skills, and teaching beading in our store, I have gained a wealth of knowledge on a wide range of beading techniques. All of these I have gathered together in this book, to provide a great reference point for anyone starting out in beading, experimenting with a new idea, or trying to master a particular technique.

The thing that inspires me most about beading is the variety of colors, textures, and materials available to experiment with. Once you become familiar with the different jewelry-making components, you have the basis to create some stunning designs, elaborate or simple.

In the techniques section you will be shown the basic bead stringing, stitching, knotting, and wirework techniques needed to start making your own beaded jewelry or expand your skills. There are then 30 projects in the book to work through, ranging from simple to advanced, showing you a variety of further techniques and inspirational ideas.

There is something here for everyone, from projects to attempt when you are just starting out, to ones for those who have already done a bit of beadwork and want to give something different a try, while learning some new techniques. The length of time needed to complete each of these projects ranges from five minutes, for the simplest jewelry, to two hours for more ambitious pieces.

By working your way through the techniques and projects in this book, you will be well on your way to creating your own beautiful jewelry.

Types of Beads

Glass Beads

There is a huge variety of beads to choose from to make some wonderful jewelry, and glass beads form the largest and most varied category.

Seed Beads

These are tiny glass beads, generally under 4mm in size, used mainly for bead stitching, weaving and embroidery. They can also be used as spacers between other beads. Seed beads are sold by size, ranging from around size 22 (the smallest), up to size 6 (the largest), with the most common sizes being 15, 11, 8, and 6 (see size chart, right). As the bead size number increases, the physical size of each bead decreases. This is because the numbers are based on the "aught" sizing system, which originally specified how many beads fitted into an inch.

Most modern high quality seed beads are made in Japan or the Czech Republic. The Japanese beads are manufactured by Matsuno, the oldest of the three Japanese seed bead manufacturers in Osaka, Toho in Hiroshima, and Miyuki in Fukuyama, Hiroshima. Preciosa is the name of the manufacturer of seed beads in the Czech Republic.

Seed Bead Sizes

Aught size	mm size
15/0	**1.5**
14/0	1.6
13/0	1.7
12/0	1.9
11/0	**2.1**
10/0	2.0
9/0	2.2
8/0	**2.5**
7/0	2.9
6/0	**3.3**

(The most common sizes are in bold type)

Seed beads come in a wide variety of shapes and sizes.

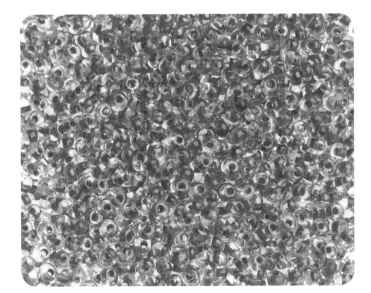

Rocailles are slightly flattened, donut-shaped seed beads.

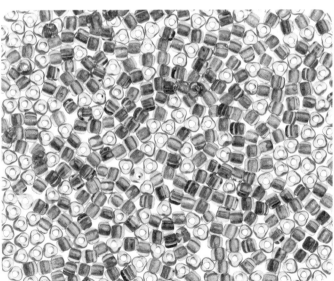

Triangular seed beads are three-dimensional triangles with rounded sides.

TYPES OF BEADS

Charlottes are faceted on one side so they reflect more light.

Cylinder beads are regular in size and shape. Their flat sides mean they sit together closely and their even sizing will make your work neat and precise. Examples are Miyuki Delicas and Toho Treasures.

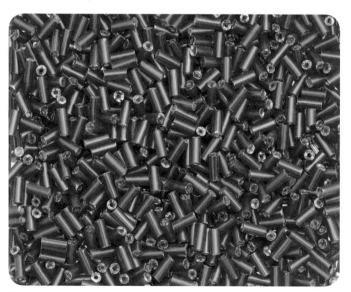

Bugle beads are long, thin tubes.

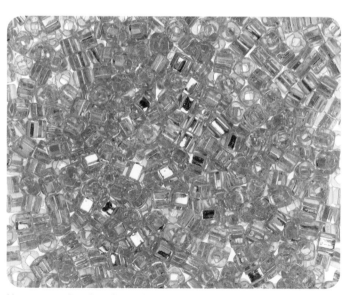

Hexagon or hex beads are tiny six-sided cylinders.

Larger Glass Beads

In addition to seed beads there are many other types of glass bead in every color and finish imaginable. Larger beads tend to be heavy, so ensure you use appropriately sturdy stringing material to take their weight.

Pressed-glass beads are made by pressing molten glass into molds. They come in many shapes and colors, and should be seamless.

Fire-polished glass beads are faceted beads that come in some beautiful colors and finishes. After they are machine cut, the beads are placed in a kiln, which melts and softens the facets.

Lampwork glass beads are made by hand. Glass is melted with a flame torch before the beads are shaped. Other handmade beads include dichroic and millefiori.

Crystal Beads

The addition of lead changes glass into crystal. When lead oxide is added to molten glass it increases the refractive index, giving lead-crystal beads much more sparkle and shine than glass beads. Full lead crystal must contain at least 24 percent lead.

A common coating for crystals is **aurora borealis (AB)**. This creates an iridescent effect onto the color of the crystal. Other coatings include: matte, vitrail, satin, and dorado.

Swarovski crystal is manufactured in Wattens, Austria and has 32 percent lead for very high quality crystal beads.

Cubic zirconia beads are made in a laboratory from a crystalline form of zirconium dioxide. They are made to look like diamonds and have brilliant sparkle and color.

Semi-precious Beads

These are either made from naturally occurring stones mined from the ground, or synthetic ones created in a laboratory. Popular semi-precious stones for beads include amethyst, aquamarine, turquoise, peridot, topaz, opal, lapis lazuli, rose quartz, rock crystal, hematite, and jade.

Natural semi-precious stones are mined, cut, and then polished into beads, and are available in a variety of sizes and shapes. They may contain imperfections.

Synthetic semi-precious stones have all the visual, chemical, and physical properties of their natural counterparts, but usually appear flawless.

Rock crystal is pure quartz and very popular, especially once it has been electroplated to give it a range of amazing colors.

Druzy stones have a glittery effect of tiny crystals over the top of a colorful mineral.

Natural Beads

Beads made from natural materials are widely available in many different shapes, colors, and sizes, including pearl, shell, wood, horn, and seeds.

Pearls

Naturally occurring pearls are expensive due to their relative rarity. The more affordable freshwater cultured pearls are created by adding an irritant to freshwater mussels, speeding up the pearl-making process. Cultured pearls typically come in white and cream, but can sometimes have a pink, peach, or lilac color to them.

Wood Beads

Wood beads are lightweight even when quite large, and particularly popular for men's jewelry. The wood can be cut and polished into many shapes and may be left natural, stained, or painted. Large, bright wood beads are great for children to learn beading techniques with as they are easy to handle yet tactile and robust.

Freshwater pearls are graded A, AA, or AAA, with AAA being the highest quality. The qualities to look for in freshwater pearls are their shape, luster, surface, nacre (or iridescence), and how well they match.

Wood beads often have larger threading holes than other beads, allowing you to string them onto a wider choice of materials, in particular leather.

Shell beads come in a wide variety of sizes. These can make the most beautiful natural beads.

Molded Beads

Rather than drilling a hole through something solid to create a bead, many beads are molded from soft materials with a hole included for stringing, and then hardened to hold their shape.

Acrylic and plastic beads are particularly great for children to make jewelry with as they are inexpensive, and come in a variety of bright colors, sizes, and shapes. High quality acrylic beads will not have seams, and they can also be electroplated in a variety of different metallic finishes.

Ceramic and porcelain beads are made from clay that is glazed and then fired in a kiln.

Polymer clay beads are made from a type of PVC-based modeling clay, so technically are plastic. These can be very decorative and colorful, and are a popular choice if you want to make your own beads.

Metal Beads

These are available in a wide variety of sizes, shapes, and surface patterns (see different types of metals on page 66), and may be pure metal or plated.

Metal beads come in all different shapes and sizes.

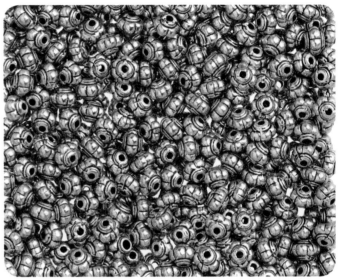

Spacer beads are typically made from metal, and are small beads used as accents in a design or to separate larger beads.

Vintage Beads

Any beads more than 25 years old would be considered as "vintage." Recycling vintage jewelry can be a really interesting way to come up with new designs. Try hunting through local thrift stores, yard sales, or vintage fairs for interesting beads.

Vintage beads can be repurposed to create unique new jewelry.

Common Bead Shapes

Beads come in a huge array of different shapes and sizes, far too many to include every type in this book. However, some examples of the more popular shapes are shown below.

Round beads are available in a range of sizes, the most popular being 4mm, 6mm, 8mm, and 10mm.

Donut beads are disc-shaped beads with large holes in the center, ideal for using with thicker stringing materials such as leather.

Rondelle beads are like squashed round beads, and are available in a variety of sizes. They can be smooth or faceted.

Briolette & teardrop beads have the hole running across the top of the bead just underneath the point of the teardrop.

Bicone beads taper to a point at each end, and popular sizes of bicone beads are 3mm, 4mm, and 6mm.

Barrel beads are cylindrical in shape, and are available in a variety of sizes, materials, and colors.

Cube beads are normally available in 4mm, 6mm, and 8mm sizes in a vast range of colors and finishes.

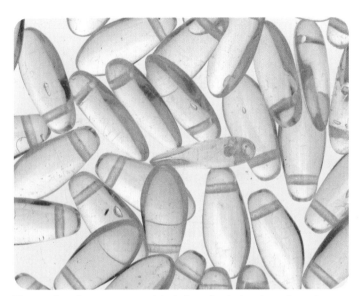

Dagger beads are a more pointed alternative to teardrop-shaped beads, with the hole running across the top of the bead.

Disc beads are like flattened round beads and sit flat when worn.

Nugget beads are slightly irregular in shape, and are a popular type of semi-precious stone or glass bead.

Oval beads are another popular shape for semi-precious stone beads, as well as glass and porcelain beads.

Jewelry Findings

Jewelry Findings

Findings are all the components needed to construct your jewelry designs besides the beads themselves. Once you know which findings are used with which stringing materials, you'll be able to create your own successful jewelry designs. Findings are usually made from metal; for more information on different types of metal see page 66.

Jump Rings and Split Rings

Jump rings are strong round or oval wire rings that twist open and closed. They are used to attach findings or connect findings to stringing material. Split rings are similar to jump rings but the wire ends overlap, and so you feed attachments between the coils and around the rings until they have reached the center.

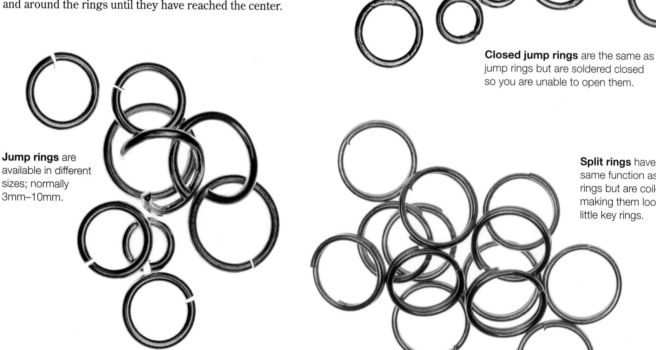

Closed jump rings are the same as jump rings but are soldered closed so you are unable to open them.

Jump rings are available in different sizes; normally 3mm–10mm.

Split rings have the same function as jump rings but are coiled, making them look like little key rings.

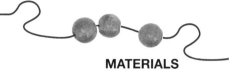

Crimp Beads, Tubes, and Covers

These are mainly used to attach clasps and jump rings onto the ends of beading wire (7 strand, 19 strand, 49 strand). Crimps can also be used to position beads along beading wire and crimpable chain. The covers are small, hollow round beads that have an opening on one side, allowing you to slide them on and over the crimp bead or tube. You can then close the crimp cover around the flattened crimp bead or tube so that it is hidden from your design, giving a more professional finish.

Crimp beads are round and available in different sizes. They can be flattened down onto beading wire using chain nose pliers.

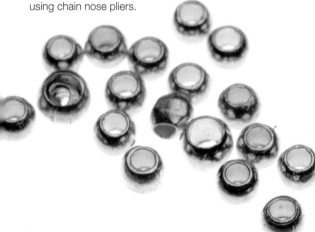

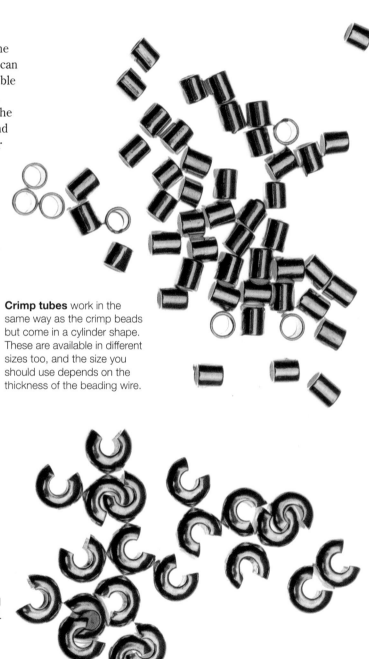

Crimp tubes work in the same way as the crimp beads but come in a cylinder shape. These are available in different sizes too, and the size you should use depends on the thickness of the beading wire.

Crimp covers are also available in different sizes to fit the size of crimp bead or tube that you have used.

Headpins and Eyepins

These are widely used in all aspects of jewelry making, and allow you to attach beads to a piece without the need to string them onto cord or thread.

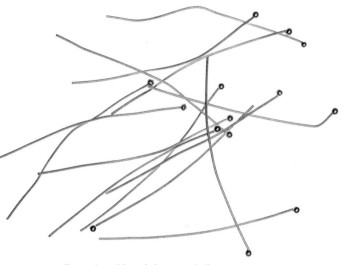

Round end headpins are similar to flat headpins but instead of having a flat stopper the end has a little rounded piece of metal, adding extra detail to your jewelry design.

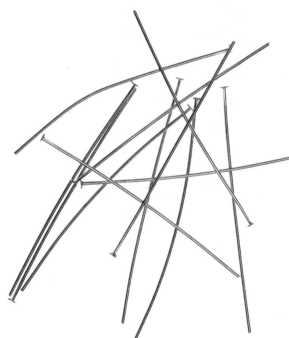

Flat headpins are pins with a flat metal disc at one end. They are used to stop beads from falling off when you are making earrings, charms, pendants, drops, or dangles.

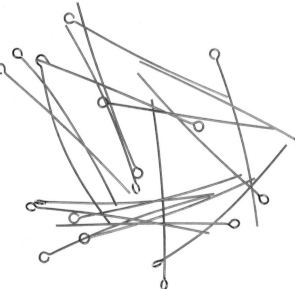

Eyepins have an eye loop at the end that keeps the beads on. The loop may have other findings or beads connected to it.

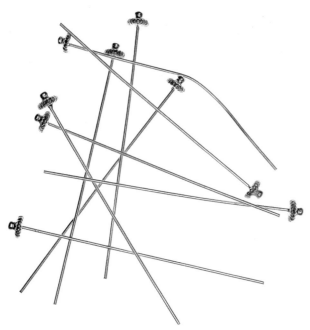

Fancy headpins have even more decorative stoppers than round end headpins.

Earring Findings

There are many types of earring findings available, and popular styles include hoops, posts, leverback, kidney, clip-on, and fish hooks (also known as French wires). The shape of earring finding you use is very much part of the design. It is worth considering using a precious metal or hypoallergenic metal when making earrings as many people are sensitive to having non-precious metals in their ears.

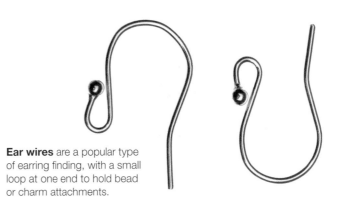

Ear wires are a popular type of earring finding, with a small loop at one end to hold bead or charm attachments.

Clasps

Any device that allows you to attach one end of a necklace or bracelet to the other end, in a temporary way, is a clasp. They can be plain or more decorative in their design, adding to the overall appearance of a piece of jewelry.

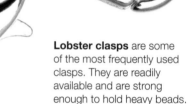

Barrel clasps consist of two textured parts that screw together to form a barrel shape. They are attached via an eye loop on either end of a necklace or bracelet.

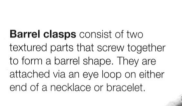

Lobster clasps are some of the most frequently used clasps. They are readily available and are strong enough to hold heavy beads.

Magnetic clasps are made from very strong magnets, making them very easy clasps to use when fastening and taking off items of jewelry.

Bolt ring clasps are readily available and commonly used on necklaces. They come in different sizes and the larger sizes are able to hold heavy beads. The clasp will stay closed until you pull back the lever, creating a space in the ring to clip on the other end of the necklace or bracelet.

Toggle clasps are made up of two pieces; a T-bar and a ring. The T-bar is fed through the ring to connect the two together.

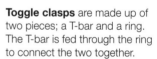

Kumihimo Beaded Bracelet page 196

Endings for Stringing Materials

For a clasp to be attached to a piece of strung jewelry, an ending of some sort needs to be added to the stringing material. The type of ending you will need depends on the stringing material.

Wire guardians are rigid metal horseshoe-shaped findings that protect and conceal stringing materials (usually beading wire), by threading the stringing materials through the horseshoe shape.

French bullion wire / French coil / gimp is a hollow tube of tightly coiled fine wire. Available in different sizes, it is used to protect soft stringing materials such as silk, from fraying.

Fold-over cord ends are used in particular to secure soft stringing material such as leather and fine chain (i.e crimpable chain). The sides are folded over the stringing material one at a time, securing the cord end in place, and a jump ring may be attached to the loop.

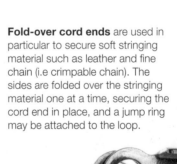

Beadtips / clam shells / calottes are threaded onto stringing material (usually silk thread) to conceal knots. The cups close around the knot, and have loops on them so that a jump ring and clasp may be attached.

Bails

These are used to turn beads into pendants so that they may be easily attached to a necklace or bracelet.

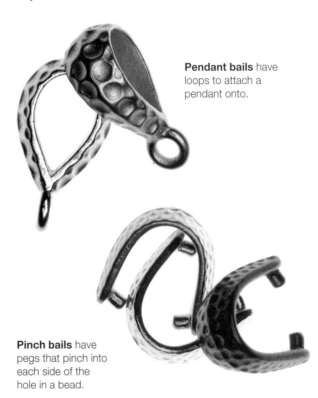

Pendant bails have loops to attach a pendant onto.

Pinch bails have pegs that pinch into each side of the hole in a bead.

Stick-on bails allow you to stick on a cabochon or other flat-back item so that it can be worn as a pendant.

Glue-in cord ends come in different sizes allowing you to glue in cord with a small amount of E-6000 glue. You would use these cord ends for leather and kumihimo braids.

Other Useful Findings

The findings you need depend, of course, on what you are making, but the examples here show some of the vast range of products available to enable your jewelry making to be simple, fast, and fun.

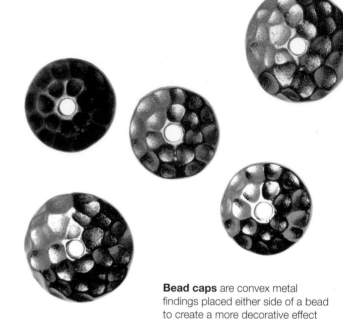

Bead caps are convex metal findings placed either side of a bead to create a more decorative effect by framing the bead. They come in a variety of sizes and designs.

End cones are perfect for hiding stringing ends and give a decorative finish to your work.

Spacer bars are flat metal bars with varying numbers of holes in them, allowing you to have multiple strands that are separated in your design.

Rainbow Cuff page 162

Flower Hairband page 178

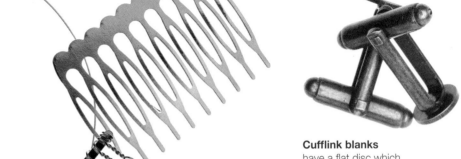

Hair combs, tiara bands, hair slides can all have beads attached to them with wire to make hair jewelry.

Cufflink blanks have a flat disc which you are able to glue flat-back beads onto with epoxy glue.

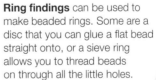

Brooch backs are available in different sizes and have holes on them allowing you to attach beads using wire.

Ring findings can be used to make beaded rings. Some are a disc that you can glue a flat bead straight onto, or a sieve ring allows you to thread beads on through all the little holes.

Extension chains can be attached to necklaces or bracelets, giving the wearer the option to change the length.

Stringing Materials

Stringing Materials

Choosing the right stringing material is key to a successful project; you need to consider which beads you are using and the size of hole that they have, and which stringing material is going to help you best achieve the design that you want.

Cords

Among the many different cords available for stringing beads is beading wire, and this is perhaps the most popular and versatile choice. It comes in three different strengths; 7 strand, 19 strand, and 49 strand, with 49 strand being the strongest. All three types are made up of thin strands of stainless steel twisted together and coated with nylon. Other good choices include nylon satin cord, leather, waxed cotton, illusion, and elastic cords.

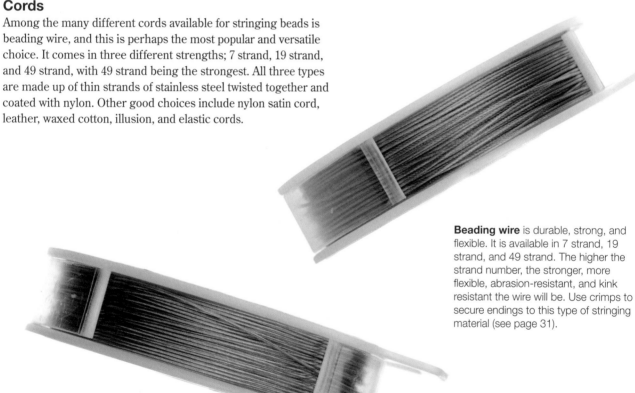

Beading wire is durable, strong, and flexible. It is available in 7 strand, 19 strand, and 49 strand. The higher the strand number, the stronger, more flexible, abrasion-resistant, and kink resistant the wire will be. Use crimps to secure endings to this type of stringing material (see page 31).

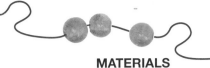

Nylon satin cord, commonly known as rat tail, has a silky, shiny surface. It is particularly good for knotting and braiding and is available in a range of bright colors. It is normally available in thicknesses of 1mm and 2mm.

Waxed cotton cord is available in many colors, ranging from 0.5mm–1mm in diameter, and is used in particular for knotting techniques (macramé). The wax helps the knots stay firmly in place and gives the jewelry a sturdier feel.

Leather cord is typically a smooth round cord, but it is also available braided or flat. It is available in a range of colors and in thicknesses from 1mm–4mm. Leather is great for hanging pendants from, or if the holes of the beads are large enough, for stringing beads directly onto the leather.

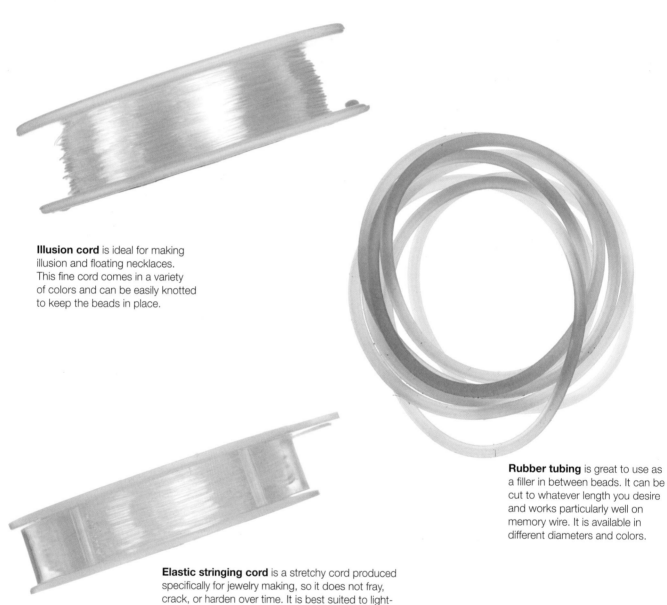

Illusion cord is ideal for making illusion and floating necklaces. This fine cord comes in a variety of colors and can be easily knotted to keep the beads in place.

Rubber tubing is great to use as a filler in between beads. It can be cut to whatever length you desire and works particularly well on memory wire. It is available in different diameters and colors.

Elastic stringing cord is a stretchy cord produced specifically for jewelry making, so it does not fray, crack, or harden over time. It is best suited to light-to medium-weight beads. It is available in different colors, the most popular being clear. It is also available in different diameters from 0.5mm–1mm. The best way to secure this stringing material is by tying a double overhand knot (see page 89).

Threads

One of the best threads for beading is natural silk, which comes in a variety of colors and thicknesses, and is usually supplied in a 2 yard length on a card with a flexible needle attached. The threads are sized by number which corresponds to their width in diameter (see the chart below). Nylon beading thread is strong and is used both for straightforward stringing and for bead stitching projects. Light and flexible, it comes in many different colors. Fine beading thread is used in bead weaving projects when the thread has to pass through tiny seed beads or delicas several times. It is stronger than sewing thread and can be easily threaded on a sharp needle.

Natural Silk Thread Widths

Size	Diameter in mm
No.0	0.30
No.1	0.35
No.2	0.45
No.3	0.50
No.4	**0.60**
No.5	0.65
No.6	**0.70**
No.7	0.75
No.8	**0.80**
No.10	0.90
No.12	0.98
No.14	1.02
No.16	**1.05**

(The most common sizes are in bold type.)

Natural silk is a strong and durable stringing material made up of tight, twisted strands of silk. It is a good choice when using semi-precious beads and pearls, as they flow better on silk and can be knotted into place. Griffin silk cord is a popular brand for this product.

Monofilament is an inexpensive clear single-strand thread. This type of cord can be secured with knots.

Elonga is thread-like elastic, and you would need to use a collapsible eye needle when threading beads onto this type of stringing material. It is secured by tying a double overhand knot (see page 89).

Nylon beading threads come in different weights, relating to the amount of force a thread can withstand without breaking. As a general rule they range from light to heavy weight: OO, O, A, B, C, D, E, F, FF, FFF. Usually the greater the thread weight, the larger the thread diameter. Nymo is a common brand of nylon thread, and is most often used with seed beads when bead stitching.

Braided nylon / polyethylene threads are another popular choice, and well-established brands of this type of thread include Fire Line, Dandyline, and Power Pro.

Weaver Bracelet page 136

Beaded wire pendant page 183

Wire

Wire for making jewelry comes in many different thicknesses, colors, and even shapes. Making jewelry from wire is known as "wirework jewelry." Wire size is determined by the diameter of the wire, given as a gauge number or in mm. The smaller the gauge, the thicker the wire. The most popular size wires are 18Ga, 20Ga, 22Ga, 26Ga, and 28Ga. See the table on page 53 for wire sizes.

Wire is also available in different shapes, including round, half-round, square, triangular, and twisted. Round shaped wire is the best shape to start out with when working with wire and as you get more experienced, you can try out different types. A popular brand of wire is Artistic Wire; it is a permanently colored copper wire that resists tarnishing, chipping, and peeling.

Wire is sold in different levels of hardness; soft, hard, and half-hard. The different hardnesses are suitable for different projects.

Soft wire is good for wrapping around another wire—it won't harden and become brittle as you work.

Hard wire is good for making clasps and weight-bearing components, as it has the strength to keep its shape. It is not suitable for wrapping or any techniques that require a lot of work as the wire will become very difficult to manipulate and too hard on your hands.

Half-hard wire is good for lots of different types of wirework as it is very versatile. Despite this versatility, do not choose this wire if you particularly need a really soft or hard wire for a project.

18Ga wire is good for making shapes to add beads to such as pendants, earrings, and rings. It can still be shaped with the hands, for example around a ring mandrel, but is thick enough to keep its shape.

20Ga wire is good for making shapes such as rings, pendants, and earrings, and can also be used for wire wrapping, creating a chunky effect. It can be used to create double ended eye loops (see page 76) and is a comfortable size to fit through the ears, so is a good size to use when making ear wires.

22Ga wire is a good size for wire wrapping, particularly when wrapping around teardrop-shaped beads to create a wrapped briolette (see page 74).

26Ga & 28Ga; these thinner wires are good for making tight coils around a thicker wire and beaded wire coiling (see page 78). They are also good for any kind of wrapping and twisting.

Wraparound Tubing Bracelet page 142

Memory wire is so named because it holds its shape. It is made from toughened steel and is available in silver, or gold-plated. It comes in necklace, bracelet, and ring sizes. Flat memory wire is also available, which allows you to wrap small beads to the surface, rather than threading the beads directly on. You need to make sure that you cut both types of memory wire with memory wire cutters—it will dent your normal cutters as the wire is so hard.

Tip
Always keep your scrap wire if you are working with precious metal as this can be collected and sold to a metal merchant.

Wire Size Chart

Gauge (Ga)	Actual diameter in mm	Rounded diameter in mm
10	2.588	2.5
11	2.035	2
12	2.053	2
13	1.828	1.75
14	1.628	1.5
15	1.450	1.5
16	1.291	1.25
17	1.150	1.2
18	**1.024**	**1**
19	0.912	0.9
20	**0.812**	**0.8**
21	0.723	0.7
22	**0.644**	**0.6**
23	0.573	0.55
24	**0.511**	**0.5**
25	0.455	0.45
26	**0.405**	**0.4**
27	0.361	0.35
28	**0.321**	**0.3**
29	0.286	0.28
30	**0.255**	**0.25**
31	0.227	0.22
32	**0.202**	**0.2**

(The most common sizes are in bold type)

Chain

Chain is usually available from bead suppliers in 1 yard lengths. These can then be cut to any length you want, and finished off by attaching jump rings to either end and a clasp.

They are ideal for hanging pendants and can also be added to each end of a beaded necklace or bracelet so that you do not have to bead all the way round.

There are many different styles of chain available in various types of metal; gold, gold-filled, gold-plated, sterling silver, silver-plated, brass, copper, gunmetal, steel, and aluminum are the most common types. Some chains will have soldered links, others will be made with links that can be opened and closed in the same way you open and close jump rings.

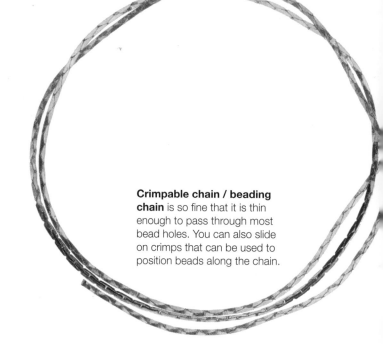

Crimpable chain / beading chain is so fine that it is thin enough to pass through most bead holes. You can also slide on crimps that can be used to position beads along the chain.

Trace chain is the simplest style of chain. The links in a trace chain are typically uniform in breadth and thickness, and can be very delicate, especially in finer widths.

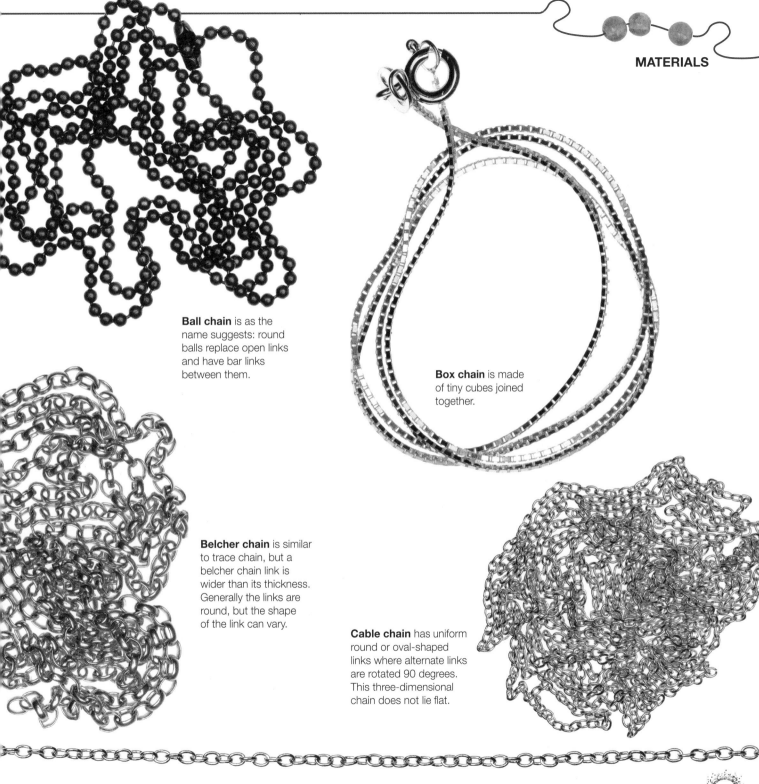

Ball chain is as the name suggests: round balls replace open links and have bar links between them.

Box chain is made of tiny cubes joined together.

Belcher chain is similar to trace chain, but a belcher chain link is wider than its thickness. Generally the links are round, but the shape of the link can vary.

Cable chain has uniform round or oval-shaped links where alternate links are rotated 90 degrees. This three-dimensional chain does not lie flat.

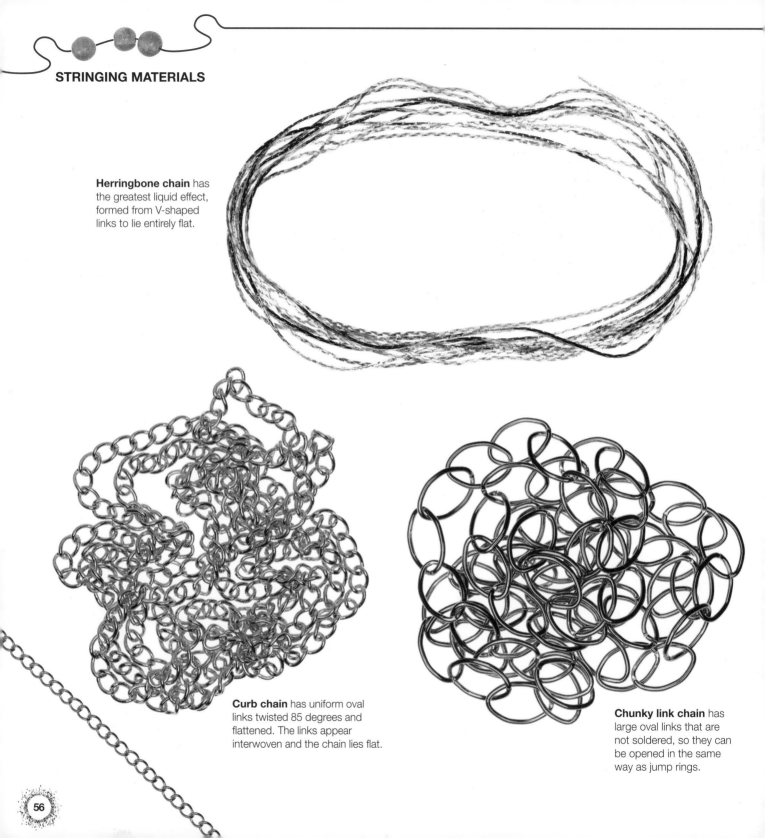

Herringbone chain has the greatest liquid effect, formed from V-shaped links to lie entirely flat.

Curb chain has uniform oval links twisted 85 degrees and flattened. The links appear interwoven and the chain lies flat.

Chunky link chain has large oval links that are not soldered, so they can be opened in the same way as jump rings.

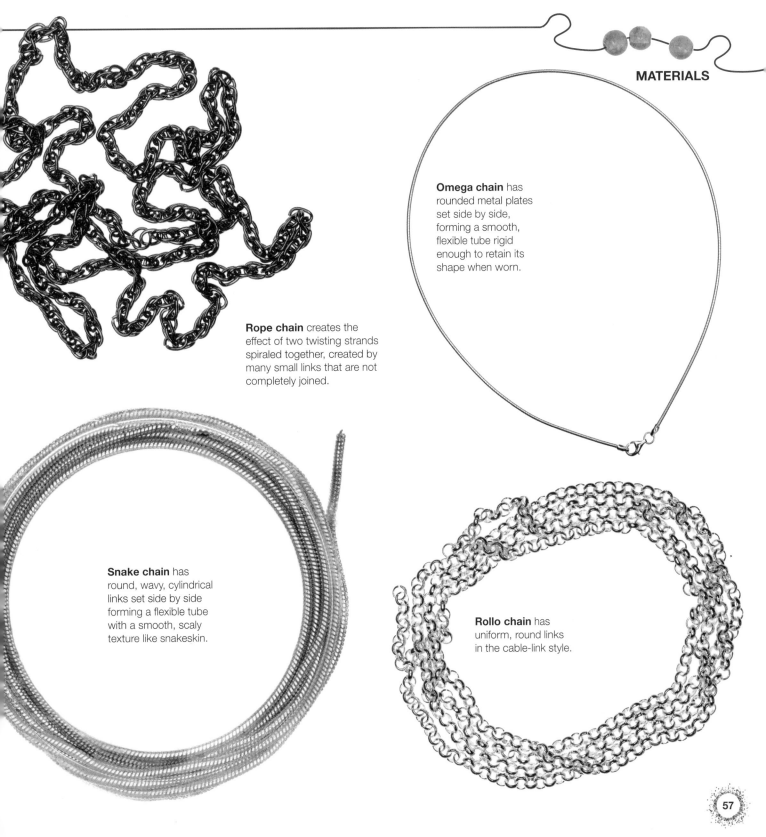

Omega chain has rounded metal plates set side by side, forming a smooth, flexible tube rigid enough to retain its shape when worn.

Rope chain creates the effect of two twisting strands spiraled together, created by many small links that are not completely joined.

Snake chain has round, wavy, cylindrical links set side by side forming a flexible tube with a smooth, scaly texture like snakeskin.

Rollo chain has uniform, round links in the cable-link style.

Tools & Information

Tools

There are four essential tools that you need for making pretty much all beaded jewelry; chain nose pliers, flat nose pliers, round nose pliers and nippers. The other useful tools and equipment listed here are needed for particular projects.

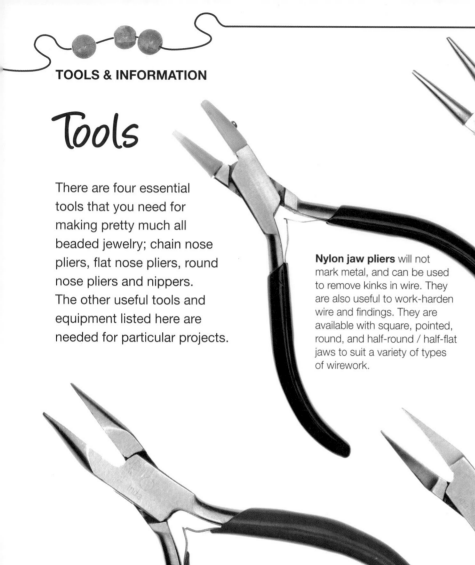

Nylon jaw pliers will not mark metal, and can be used to remove kinks in wire. They are also useful to work-harden wire and findings. They are available with square, pointed, round, and half-round / half-flat jaws to suit a variety of types of wirework.

Round nose pliers have completely round, smooth tapered jaws. They are used to bend wire into loops of various sizes, depending on where you position the wire on the jaw of the pliers. These are an essential tool when making earrings and many other jewelry designs.

Chain nose pliers are the most versatile type, ideal for gripping and bending wire, crimping, wire wrapping, opening jump rings, closing clamshells, and pinching in and tidying up the ends of wire. They have a short needle nose and flat closing surface. Make sure the inside of your tool is smooth and not ridged, as this type will make marks and dents on your findings.

Flat nose pliers can perform similar functions to chain nose pliers but they have a rectangular jaw. They are most useful to use with chain nose pliers when opening and closing jump rings.

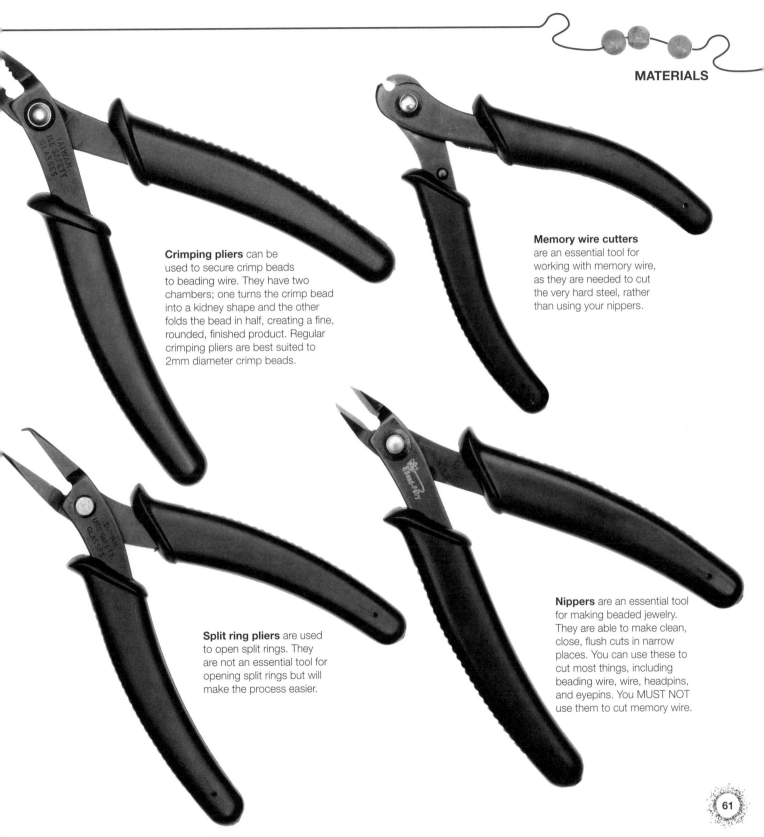

Crimping pliers can be used to secure crimp beads to beading wire. They have two chambers; one turns the crimp bead into a kidney shape and the other folds the bead in half, creating a fine, rounded, finished product. Regular crimping pliers are best suited to 2mm diameter crimp beads.

Memory wire cutters are an essential tool for working with memory wire, as they are needed to cut the very hard steel, rather than using your nippers.

Split ring pliers are used to open split rings. They are not an essential tool for opening split rings but will make the process easier.

Nippers are an essential tool for making beaded jewelry. They are able to make clean, close, flush cuts in narrow places. You can use these to cut most things, including beading wire, wire, headpins, and eyepins. You MUST NOT use them to cut memory wire.

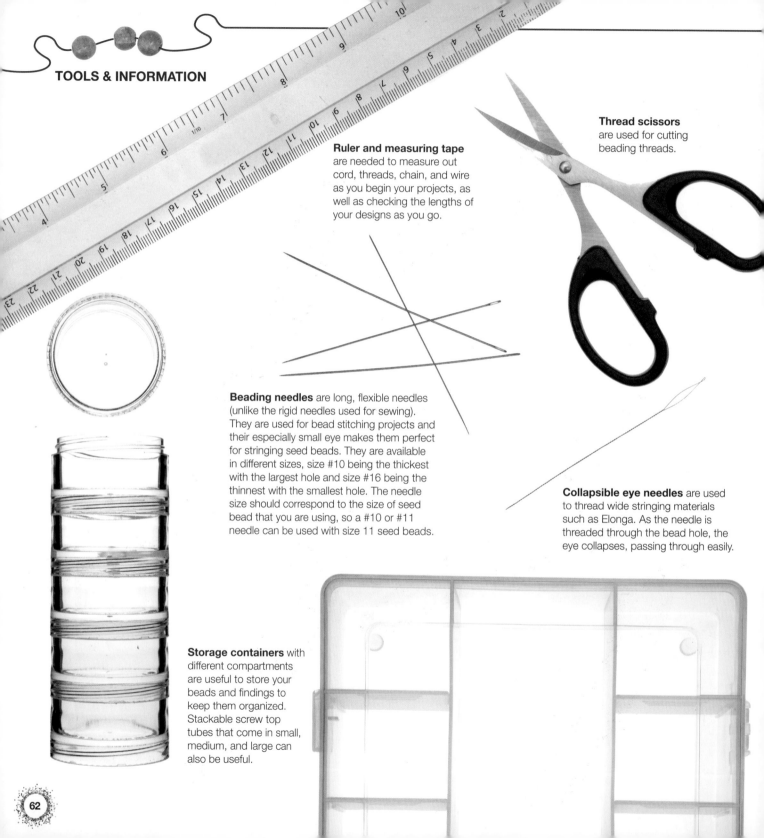

Ruler and measuring tape are needed to measure out cord, threads, chain, and wire as you begin your projects, as well as checking the lengths of your designs as you go.

Thread scissors are used for cutting beading threads.

Beading needles are long, flexible needles (unlike the rigid needles used for sewing). They are used for bead stitching projects and their especially small eye makes them perfect for stringing seed beads. They are available in different sizes, size #10 being the thickest with the largest hole and size #16 being the thinnest with the smallest hole. The needle size should correspond to the size of seed bead that you are using, so a #10 or #11 needle can be used with size 11 seed beads.

Collapsible eye needles are used to thread wide stringing materials such as Elonga. As the needle is threaded through the bead hole, the eye collapses, passing through easily.

Storage containers with different compartments are useful to store your beads and findings to keep them organized. Stackable screw top tubes that come in small, medium, and large can also be useful.

Bead stoppers are little springs available in small and large sizes, and clip onto your stringing material to stop the beads coming off one end. These are particularly useful for children to use when making elasticated bracelets and necklaces.

Adhesives are available for all kinds of beading materials. Hypo-cement comes with a very fine tip, so is ideal for dabbing a little onto knots to give them some extra security. E-6000 is ideal to use for gluing leather, braids, etc. into cord ends. Two-part Epoxy is incredibly strong, dries clear, and is used when a larger surface needs to be glued, for example attaching flat-backed beads to cufflink and ring blanks. It will hold metal, glass, crystal, wood, and many other materials. Fabric glue dries clear and is useful for soutache jewelry.

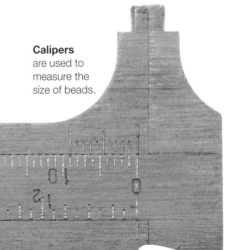

Beeswax / thread conditioner is used to condition beading thread. Beeswax makes the thread stronger and stiffer (to help maintain tension), it also keeps out moisture and prevents tangles. Thread conditioner is a synthetic alternative to beeswax that also strengthens thread and wards off tangles but is less sticky than wax.

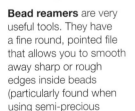

Bead reamers are very useful tools. They have a fine round, pointed file that allows you to smooth away sharp or rough edges inside beads (particularly found when using semi-precious beads). They can also be used to make a bead hole slightly bigger and to dislodge any obstruction inside the bead hole.

Calipers are used to measure the size of beads.

Bead mats provide a flocked surface that is essential for laying beads out on when planning a design as it stops the beads from rolling away.

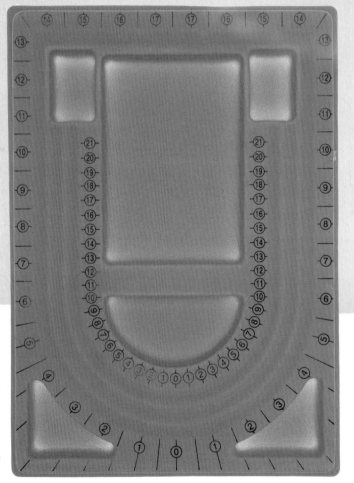

Ring mandrels are special tapered wooden poles needed when making beaded wire rings. You can slide on a ring sizer and mark the mandrel with a pencil where you need to wrap the wire around to make your ring. They are tapered, and you can use the bottom of the mandrel (the larger end) for shaping wire into larger shapes such earrings and pendants.

Bead design boards can help in the design of a project because you can lay out your beads on the board for single and multi-strand necklaces and bracelets before you string them. They have multiple grooves that are molded into the plastic, with a flocked surface to keep the beads in place. They are also marked with measurements so that you can see how many beads you need for a particular piece of jewelry.

Ring sizers comprise of a group of rings of fractionally different diameters, used to determine ring size. Once the appropriate ring has been located on the sizer, it can be put onto the ring mandrel to mark where the wire needs to be wrapped around. Some adjustments may need to be made depending on the style of ring that you are making.

Bobbins that clip open and closed allow you to wrap braiding cords around them when making kumihimo braids so that they do not become tangled up underneath the board.

Kumihimo boards are made of foam and have notches around the outer edge which are used to position the braiding threads. Once you begin crossing your threads over each other the braid will begin to come out through the central hole. Boards are available in round or square shapes, and large or small sizes.

Macramé board and T-pins consist of a rectangular foam board with notches around the edges, and T-shaped pins used to stick into the board, securing your work while you knot, keeping the tension tight.

Types of Metal

The many different finishes available for metal findings, beads, wire, and chain can be quite overwhelming. The metals used in making beaded jewelry can be divided into two categories: base metals and precious metals. Jewelry making materials are available in various combinations of these metals created by a number of different processes.

Base Metals

Metals and alloys in this group include the following products.

Copper: a base metal with a pink-gold color that tarnishes quickly; it can, however, be polished back to its original color very easily. It is extremely durable and easy to work with. It is often plated with sterling silver.

Brass: an alloy made from 70 percent copper and 30 percent zinc.

Pewter: an alloy of 85–90 percent tin with the balance consisting of copper, antimony, and lead. Lead-free pewter is now available (as used in TierraCast products). Pewter has an appealing antiqued silver-gray color.

Niobium: a completely hypoallergenic, tarnish-resistant base metal. Ideal for using when making earrings as many people are sensitive to having metal in their ears. It is a great option for people who are allergic to other metals, including precious metals.

Gold- / Silver-plated metals: these have a very thin layer of precious metal plated onto the surface of a base metal. The plating is usually not very durable and the finish can chip off or wear away, but this is reflected in the price.

Precious Metals

Precious metals are rare metals of high economic value, namely platinum, gold, and silver. As well as their pure forms, they are available as the following products.

Gold filled: this looks like fine gold but is less expensive as it is made by bonding a thick layer of 10 to 18 karat gold to a brass base. Gold filled items are hypoallergenic and the gold will not wear off or tarnish.

Vermeil: this is made by plating at least 10 karat gold onto sterling silver. It has a thicker layer of gold plated onto it than standard plating but not as thick as gold filled. Vermeil has the richness and shine of gold that won't wear off or tarnish.

Fine silver: this is 99.9 percent pure silver and doesn't tarnish easily. Wire made from fine silver is slightly softer than dead-soft sterling silver wire.

Sterling silver: is an alloy made from 92.5 percent silver and 7.5 percent copper. Copper actually strengthens the silver, making it harder, stronger, and easier to work with than fine silver. Sterling silver does oxidize though, which means it will need to be polished to remove any tarnish that appears. Sterling silver is also hypoallergenic.

Jewelry Size Guide

The table below is a guide only; remember that lengths may appear longer or shorter depending on the wearer.

Size Guide

Type of jewelry	length in inches	length in centimeters
Collar necklace	12–13	30–33
Choker necklace	14–16	35.5–40.5
Princess necklace	17–19	43–48
Matinee necklace	20–24	50–61
Opera necklace	28–35	71–89
Rope necklace	40–45	102–114
Lariat necklace	48+	122+
Small bracelet	6½–7	16.5–18
Medium bracelet	7–8	18–20
Large / men's bracelet	8–9	20–23
Small anklet	9	23
Medium anklet	10	25.5
Large anklet	11	28

Wire Techniques

Loops

Loops are crucial in beaded jewelry making as they are needed for the attachment of beads to findings. A wrapped loop gives a more secure finish to a bead attachment.

Simple Loop

This is a basic wirework technique but is extremely useful. It will enable you to make earrings, turn beads into charms or pendants, and join components together.

1 Thread your chosen bead onto a headpin or eyepin. Bend the wire to the side, creating a 45-degree angle.

2 Grip the wire with round nose pliers, and bend the wire up and over the top jaw of the pliers.

3 When you can wrap the wire around no more, remove the pliers from the loop and reinsert the lower jaw of the pliers. Continue bending the wire round to complete the loop.

4 Trim off any excess wire with nippers.

Opening a Simple Loop on an Ear Wire

Many ear wires have a simple loop on them that can be opened to hang a bead or charm from.

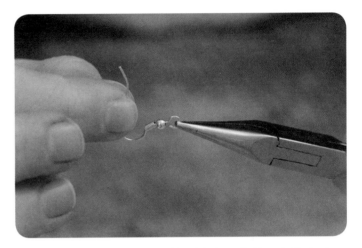

With chain nose pliers grip the side of the loop that is not attached to the main ear wire. Twist the pliers toward you slightly, opening up the loop a little. Thread your chosen wired bead or charm onto the opened loop, grip it once more with chain nose pliers and then twist the pliers away from you to close the loop.

5 With chain nose pliers pull the loop back a little so that it sits centrally on top of the headpin. You can open and close the loop you have just made by gripping one half of the loop with chain nose pliers and twisting them slightly toward you. Reverse this action to close the loop again.

Tip

The further up the round nose pliers that you make the loop, the larger the loop will be. If you want to create a very small loop, use the very tip of your tool to bend the wire around.

Wrapped Loop

This is a progression on the simple loop technique. Wrapped loops are more decorative, more secure, and add a more professional finish to your jewelry.

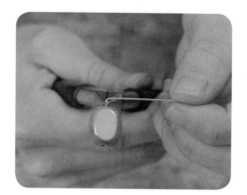

1 Slide a bead onto a headpin or eyepin. Grip the wire with chain nose pliers directly above the bead. Bend the wire over at 90 degrees directly above the pliers, creating a right-angled bend a little way above the bead.

2 Take the round nose pliers and grip the wire so that the lower jaw of the pliers sits in the bend made in the previous step, and the upper jaw grips the wire beyond the bend. Pull the wire up and over the upper jaw of pliers, bringing the wire all the way around until it hits the lower jaw of the pliers.

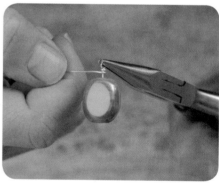

3 To complete the loop, remove the round nose pliers from the half loop you have made and insert the lower jaw into the loop. You will now be able to bend the wire around to complete the loop.

4 Grip the loop with chain nose pliers and wrap the wire around and back down toward the bead.

5 Snip off any excess wire with nippers, and pinch the end in with chain nose pliers, so that it is tucked in neatly.

Joining Wrapped Loops

Unlike simple loops, wrapped loops can no longer be opened. This means that you have to remember to add whatever you want to attach before you begin making the wraps back down toward the bead. To do this, slide your attachment onto the wire and into the loop at the point when you have completed the loop, and then grip the loop with the attachment hanging down, and begin making wraps back down toward the bead.

Loop Orientation

Often the orientation of the loops you create won't matter, but there are occasions when it will affect the way your jewelry looks. If you are making earrings or a pendant, or if your bead has a specific front or back, you will need to think about how it hangs.

1 For a front to back loop, begin bending the wire at the top of the bead from front to back.

Loops for flat pendants, for example, should always be twisted so that they sit front to back on top of the pendant, allowing the cord or chain to align side to side with the pendant. This means that the pendant can lie flat on the wearer's chest.

Loops for attachment to ear wires, however, will need to align side to side with the bead rather than front to back, so that the beads face forward when the earrings are worn.

2 The finished front to back loop allows the bead to lie flat when threaded onto a necklace.

Wrapped Briolette

This is a decorative wire wrapping technique used on teardrop-shaped beads where the hole runs across the top of the bead (briolettes). It is best to use 22Ga wire when practicing this technique, but once you have gotten to grips with it you could experiment with wires in different thicknesses.

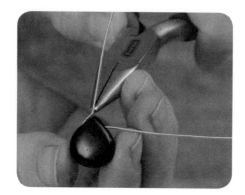

1 Take a length of 22Ga wire roughly 12in long, and slide a teardrop bead onto the wire, positioning it around 3in from one end. Bring the shorter length of wire up to the top of the teardrop and with chain nose pliers bend it back on itself slightly so that it sits upright on the top of the bead. This forms the stem wire.

2 Bring the longer length of wire up to the top of the bead and across the front of the stem.

3 Wrap the long wire around the stem wire once, and then continue to wrap the wire carefully back down the bead until the holes at each side have been covered with wire.

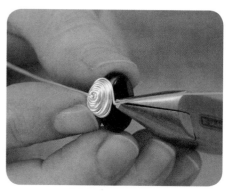

4 When you have made enough wraps with the wire, pull it back toward you and push against the bead with chain nose pliers, so that it will sit as flush as possible with the bead when the excess is trimmed off.

5 Cut off any excess wire and pinch the end in with chain nose pliers. Push the stem wire back against the coils, bending it slightly away from you. Grip the wire with round nose pliers close to the top coil.

6 Bring the wire up and over the top of your pliers, all the way around as far as it will go.

7 Now take the pliers out of the half loop you have made and reinsert the lower jaw of the pliers. Continue to bring the wire all the way around to make a complete loop.

8 Grip the loop with chain nose pliers and wrap the excess wire back down and around until it meets the wraps at the top of the bead. Cut off any excess and pinch the end in with chain nose pliers.

Double Ended Wrapped Eye Loop

This technique is useful when you want to connect two or more beads together. You can use 26–20Ga wire for this technique.

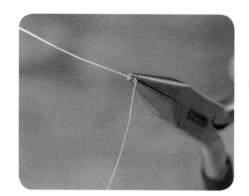

1 Take an 8in length of wire. At 2in from one end make a right-angled bend in the wire with chain nose pliers.

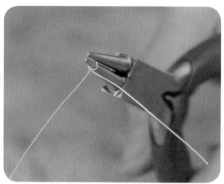

2 Create a simple loop (see page 70) in the shorter part of the wire, next to the bend. Grasp the loop with chain nose pliers and wrap the short end of the wire back down the longer length beneath the loop, however many times you need depending on the length of connector you are creating.

3 Trim away any excess wrapping wire with nippers. Use chain nose pliers to squeeze the cut end flush against the straight stem wire. Thread on a bead, grasp the wire above the bead with chain nose pliers, and bend the wire above the pliers 90 degrees.

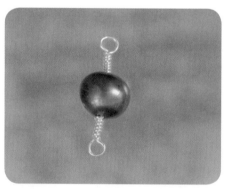

4 Grip the wire just above the bend with round nose pliers and make a wrapped loop (see page 72), wrapping the wire back down toward the bead. Trim away any excess wire and use chain nose pliers to squeeze the cut end flush against the stem.

Further Wirework Techniques

As well as creating loops above beads so that they can be attached together, thinner wire may also be used more decoratively, either threaded with beads to wrap around a frame, or to create beaded bails for large beads.

Wire Bails

Bails are a decorative way of allowing you to hang beads from a necklace. They can be plain or with added bead accents for more detail. This method can be used with teardrop-shaped beads (briolettes) or round beads. The type of bail shown here allows the beads to move, so it is important to leave a small amount of space between the top of the bead and the point where the wires cross over. 26Ga wire works best with this technique.

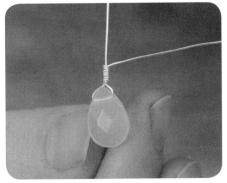

1 Take a 4in length of 26Ga wire, and slide on a bead to the halfway point of the wire. Bend the wire at each side of the bead up toward the top of the bead so that they cross over at the top center. Use chain nose pliers to bend the wire at the back straight up at the point where the wires cross, directly above the top of the bead. This is the stem wire.

2 Begin wrapping the other wire around and up the stem for about ¼in. Trim off the excess wrapping wire with nippers, but don't cut the stem wire. Use chain nose pliers to squeeze the cut wire end flush against the stem wire.

3 If you are adding an accent bead, thread it on so that it sits above the wrapped wire. Make a wrapped loop above the accent bead, or above the wrapped wire, (see page 72) to finish.

Beaded Wire Coiling

This technique is used to decorate wire structures with beads. You need to use thin 26Ga wire for this technique and it works best when used to decorate thicker wires—20Ga and above—with 2mm–4mm beads.

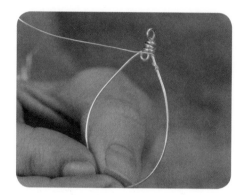

1 Take the wire structure you wish to decorate (in this case a pendant frame) and a 1 yard length of 26Ga wire. Secure the 26Ga wire to the wire structure by making a couple of coils around it, tightly but spaced apart.

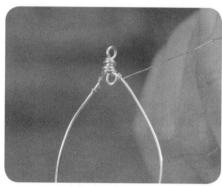

2 Continue securing the thinner wire with a few more coils—in this example the wire is taken to the top of the pendant frame, once around the stem wire at the top and across to the other side.

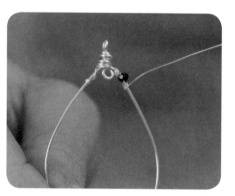

3 Once the wire is secure, pinch the end in with chain nose pliers so it is flush with the frame. Now make two tight coils with the 26Ga wire and thread on a small bead. Hold it in place against the wire frame and make two more tight coils directly after it.

4 Continue in this way until you have worked all the way around, covering the initial coils made when you first attached the wire. Secure the wire by making a couple of coils on the frame where the end can be hidden, such as the base of the stem. Cut off the excess at the back and pinch the cut end in with chain nose pliers.

Jewelry Closures

Many of the pieces of jewelry you make will require some sort of opening and closing mechanism so that the item may be worn. Get these elements right for professional jewelry that will last for many years.

Opening and Closing Jump Rings and Chain Links

Jump rings need to be opened and closed in a specific way so the metal isn't weakened and the jump ring retains its shape. The same applies to links on chains where the join isn't soldered together.

1 Using chain nose pliers grip one side of the jump ring, and grip the other side with flat nose pliers, so that the join is between the two tools.

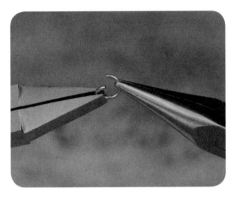

2 Gently bend your wrists in opposite directions, so that one side of the jump ring moves toward you and the other side away from you, opening the ring slightly.

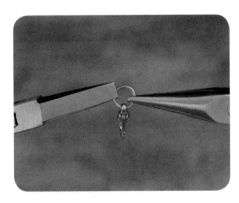

3 Release your grip on one of the pairs of pliers, add the required finding to the jump ring, or attach it to the end of your piece of jewelry. Grip with both pliers and reverse the bending action to close the jump ring. If the ends don't quite meet, try making little backward and forward motions with the pliers, whilst applying pressure to push the ring together.

4 The links on some chains are not soldered, which means they can be opened and closed like a jump ring. You can either attach beads or a clasp to the chain in this way. When adding a clasp simply allow it to dangle freely once added to the link while closing the link up again.

Attaching Clasps with Fold-over Cord Ends

When you want to attach a clasp to leather or crimpable chain, one of the easiest and quickest ways is to use fold-over cord ends. You need to make sure you are using the correct size fold-over cord end for the thickness of leather or chain.

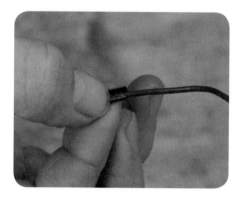

1 Place one end of the cord into the fold-over cord end, so that the end butts up to the loop at the top of the cord end.

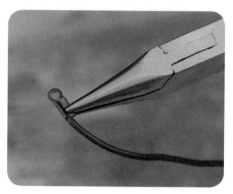

2 With the tip of the chain nose pliers, carefully bend over one side of the cord end, trapping the cord underneath it.

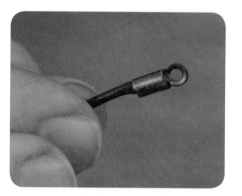

3 Repeat step 2 with the other side of the cord end, so that both sides lay as flat as possible on top of the cord. Squeeze the cord end with chain nose pliers all down the length to ensure it is held tightly in place.

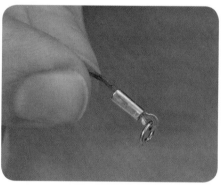

4 If you are attaching the cord end to crimpable chain, a much smaller fold-over cord end should be used.

Creating Wire Endings on Leather Cord

If you do not want to use a fold-over cord to attach a clasp to leather you can create an attachment by using 20Ga wire.

1 Take a 6in length of 20Ga wire. Place the chain nose pliers 1in from one end of the wire and make a 90-degree bend. Create a loop here with round nose pliers, add one half of your clasp, and continue to make a wrapped loop (see page 72). Cut off any excess wrapping wire, and pinch the end in to the stem wire with chain nose pliers.

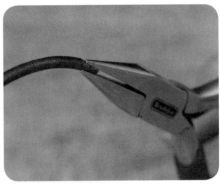

2 Flatten one end of the leather cord with chain nose pliers.

3 Position the flattened end of the leather up close to the bottom coil of the wrapped loop. Holding the wire against the leather with one hand, take the stem wire with your free hand and wrap it around the leather cord very firmly.

4 Continue wrapping the wire around the leather cord end, coiling it back up toward the clasp, keeping the coils tight. When you reach the bottom coil of the wrapped loop, cut off any excess wire and pinch the end in with chain nose pliers.

How to Use Crimp Beads, Tubes, and Covers

It is important to know how these work, as they are essential for attaching clasps to the ends of beading wire (7 strand, 19 strand, or 49 strand). If you are using crimp beads or tubes to position beads along beading wire or crimpable chain experiment with which shape and size to use; they will become part of the design as they will be visible. Crimp beads flatten into little rectangle shapes, whereas the tubes flatten into squares.

Attaching a Jump Ring or Clasp to Beading Wire

Crimps are available as round beads or tubes. It doesn't matter which style you use when using a crimp cover, as the cover will hide the bead or tube. You just need to make sure that the inner diameter of the crimp bead or tube is large enough for the beading wire to pass through twice, and that the crimp cover is large enough to cover the bead or tube. To attach a clasp instead of a jump ring, follow the method shown, but instead of sliding on a jump ring in the first step, slide a clasp onto the beading wire.

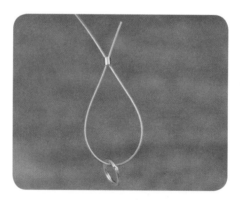

1 Take a length of beading wire, thread on a crimp bead or tube and position it roughly 2in from one end. We used a crimp tube for the photographs. Thread on a jump ring, then pass the short end of the beading wire back through the crimp tube, trapping the jump ring in the resulting loop.

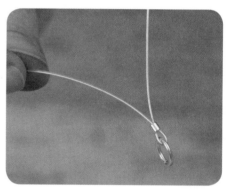

2 Slide the crimp tube up toward the jump ring so that the loop is fairly tight, but there is still enough space around the crimp tube to attach a crimp cover.

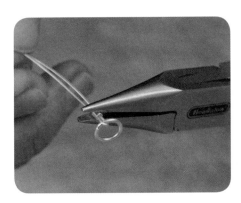

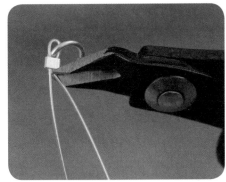

3 Make sure the wires inside the crimp tube are parallel and not crossing over. Use chain nose pliers to squeeze the crimp tube, flattening it. Work the tool backward and forward over the crimp tube, so that the beading wire is held securely in place.

4 Pull the shorter length of wire out to one side of the flattened crimp tube, and snip off the excess with nippers as close to the crimp tube as possible.

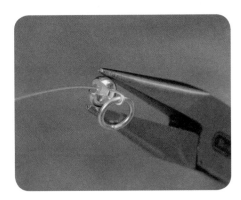

5 Choose a crimp cover large enough to fit over your crimp tube. Grip the crimp cover with chain nose pliers with the opening facing outward, and position it so that the crimp tube is sitting inside. Gently squeeze the crimp cover closed over the crimp tube; you will find that the crimp cover closes almost completely, but not quite.

6 Move your chain nose pliers so that the jaws are at the top and bottom of the crimp cover and give it a couple more gentle squeezes; you should find that this helps the edges of the crimp cover to meet. Use the pliers to give the crimp cover little squeezes here and there where needed to mold the cover around the crimp tube.

Tip
The most important thing to watch out for when attaching a crimp cover is that the beading wire does not get caught in between the edges of the crimp cover, as this could cause the wire to break. The wires need to sit neatly back within the crimp cover.

Positioning Beads with Crimps

If you want to position beads at regular intervals along a piece of beading wire or crimpable chain, then it can be helpful to have a ruler at the edge of the beading mat.

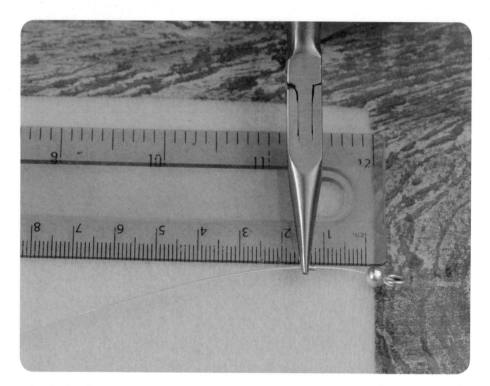

Lay the beading wire or crimpable chain onto a beading mat, alongside the ruler if using. Thread on beads with crimp beads or tubes in between according to the jewelry design. Position the beads and slide the crimp beads or tubes into place alongside with chain nose pliers, holding gently so you don't flatten the bead or tube at this stage. Once in position, flatten the crimp bead or tube with chain nose pliers so that it holds the decorative bead in the correct position.

Working with Memory Wire

You can use memory wire to make rings, bracelets, or necklaces. It is available in different sizes, colors, and shapes. Once you have decided on the shape and size that you want to use, you need to create secure endings so that your beads stay on.

Cutting Memory Wire

Memory wire is made from toughened steel, and comes supplied as a large coil with a specified number of "wraps" on the coil. It is important that you use special memory wire cutters when working with it. Ordinary nippers will become dented if you try to cut memory wire with them.

How to Create a Secure Ending

Before you begin adding your beads to the memory wire, you need to make a simple loop, so that the beads don't fall off. When you make the loops, ensure they sit on the outside of the bracelet, necklace, or ring, so that it is comfortable to wear.

1 Grip the very end of the piece of memory wire for your jewelry design with round nose pliers. Turn the pliers so that the cut end of the wire loops around the jaw until it touches the rest of the wire. You will need to be quite firm with the wire as it will be tough to loop around. If you can't create a full loop in one go, keep using the tool to work the wire until the loop is complete.

2 Thread on the beads for your jewelry design. When you reach the end of your piece you will need to leave 3/8in wire bare. Repeat step 1 to create a loop at the end of the wire to hold the beads in place.

3 It can be more attractive to add a couple of dangles to these securing loops, with the same beads you have used in the design. To make a dangle, thread a bead onto a headpin, create a wrapped loop (see page 72), and thread onto the end of the memory wire before making the secure ending loops.

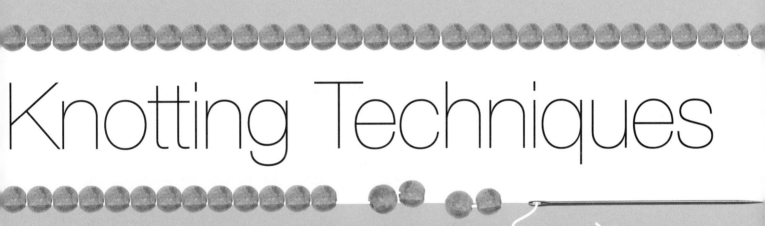

Knotting Techniques

Knotting Techniques

Knots can be used in beaded jewelry making purely for function—to hold beads in the correct position—or more decoratively, adding texture and interest to the piece. Experiment with different knots on different stringing materials for a whole host of design possibilities.

Overhand Knot

This is a very simple knot, created by making a loop in one strand of thread or cord and passing the end through. It is very useful for positioning beads along silk thread.

Make a loop with your desired thread or cord at the position you want the knot to be. Bring the end of the cord through the loop, pull a little to make the loop smaller, repositioning if necessary. Once it is in position pull tight on the thread or cord ends to secure the knot.

Double Overhand Knot

When making jewelry with elastic it is important that the knot to tie the ends together is made properly, so that is does not come undone when the elastic is stretched. The best way of tying elastic is to use a double overhand knot, and the trick is to pull it really, really tight.

1 Once you have added the beads onto the elastic cord for the jewelry design, align the two ends of the elastic and wrap them around your middle and index finger.

2 Take both ends of elastic up, around, and through the loop you have created, twice.

3 As you pull the ends of the elastic the loop should slide back toward your beads.

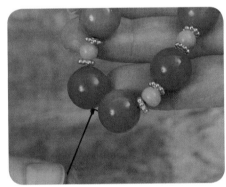

4 When the loop is up close to the beads, this is when you need to pull the ends really tight so the elastic almost gels together at the knot.

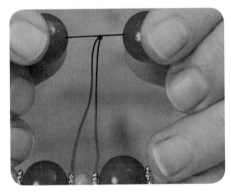

5 To test the knot, pull your elastic apart in opposite directions. If the knot unravels at all, then it has not been done correctly. If this happens start again, and ensure you pull the ends even more tightly.

Square Knot

Also known as the flat knot, this type of knot consists of two opposite half knots. It is probably one of the most popular knots used in macramé. As a rough guide, your cord should be four times the length of your finished project.

Tip

When practicing this knot for the first time, it helps if your left, right, and middle (core) threads are different colors.

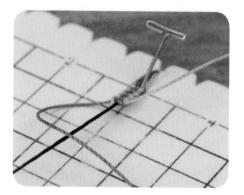

1 Attach three lengths of cord to a macramé board with a T-pin, leaving a 6in tail. Tie the first half of the square knot by bringing the left cord over the middle ("core" or "filler") cord, making an "L" shape.

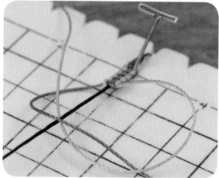

2 Bring the right cord over the tail of the left cord, then under the middle cord and up through the loop made by the left cord.

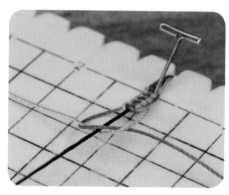

3 Pull the left and right thread tight around the core to secure.

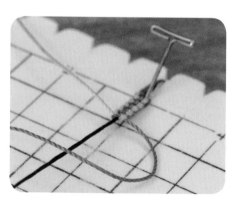

4 To make the second half of the square knot starting on the right, bring the right thread over the core, making a "C" shape.

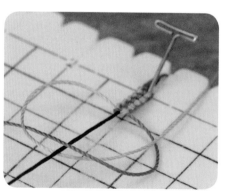

5 Bring the left cord over the tail of the right, under the core, and back up through the loop made by the right cord.

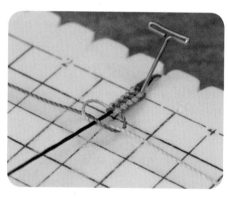

6 Pull the left and right cords tight around the core, pushing the knot up so that it sits snugly underneath the first half knot that you made.

Sliding Square Knot

A square knot made into a sliding knot, which can be useful if you do not wish to use a clasp, or want the size of what you are making to be adjustable. It works particularly well with leather and thicker cords.

1 Take the two cords you wish to slide, and an additional 20in length of cord. Hold the center of the 20in cord underneath the two cords that need to slide against each other.

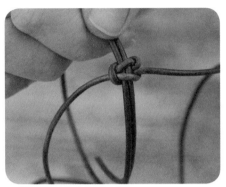

2 Begin making square knots with the 20in cord around the sliding cords, as if they are your core cord. Getting the first knot in place feels quite awkward but once it is in place it then becomes easier.

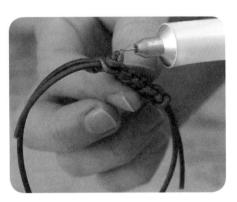

3 When you have done around 5 square knots, or have a section of knots measuring around 1¼in, you can stop and tie off the two ends of the sliding knot. Trim them back and apply a small amount of hypo cement glue on and around the knot to secure in place.

4 If you are making a sliding knot on a bracelet you will need to open up the bracelet so that it slides on over your hand. Once you have it set at the correct size, tie the ends of the bracelet right back to where they meet the sliding knot, trim back and again apply a small amount of hypo cement glue on and around the knot to secure in place. Let the glue dry for a good few hours before you move the cords through the sliding knot.

Lark's Head Knot

This knot is used to attach or mount a cord to a holding cord, ring, or other support.

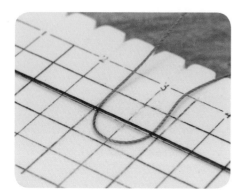

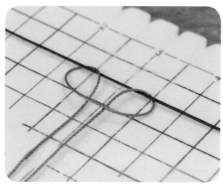

1 Fold a cord in half to create a loop, then bring the loop under the holding cord.

2 Bring the ends of the cord through the loop.

3 Pull the ends snugly over the holding cord to finish.

Lark's Head Sennit

This is a row of lark's head knots tied vertically over one or more cords to form a chain, or sennit. Two separate loops are used. The first loop passes over the core cord, then under the core and through. The second loop passes under the core cord, then over the core and through.

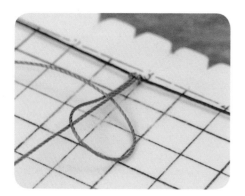

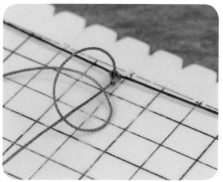

1 Tie a lark's head knot to a holding cord, or if you already have two cords, bring one of them up and over the other (the core cord). Loop it under the core and out through the loop. This forms the first half of the knot. Pull the loop snug against the core cord.

2 To tie the second half, bring the working cord under the core cord this time, looping it over the core and through.

3 To create the chain, you always tie the first half of the knot over the core cord and the second half of the knot under the core.

Crystal Macramé Bracelet page 146

Braiding and Stringing Techniques

There are many ways to string beads together, and the techniques included here form just a small selection of popular and useful methods for creating interesting effects with your cords and beads.

Simple Kumihimo Braiding

Kumihimo is a Japanese form of braiding, and "Kumi himo" is Japanese for "gathered threads." Kumihimo braids were originally created using a form of finger-loop braiding. However, Kumihimo boards are now readily available and it has become a technique popular with beaders. It is easy to learn, and there are many different patterns to experiment with.

Kumihimo boards are made from a firm but flexible foam plastic with 32 notches. They are lightweight and portable. Many different types of braids can be made using the boards, depending on where you position the strands on the board, and beads can also be incorporated into the braid. The nylon cord usually used for Kumihimo braiding is usually referred to as "rat tail" and comes in many different colors. As a guide you will always need to begin with cords four times the length of the finished braid.

1 Take four 47in lengths of rat tail. Fold them in half and tie them together at the halfway point with a small amount of thread.

2 Position the tied center of the bunch of threads over the central hole on the kumihimo board. While holding in place, arrange the 8 separate threads so that there is one each side of the four compass points on the board ("N," "E," "S," "W").

3 Once the threads are in position, have the "N" at the top. Take the cord to the right of the "N" (between 32 and 1) and bring it down to the slot to the right of the bottom right cord (between 14 and 15).

4 Take the bottom left cord (between 16 and 17) to the slot to the left of the top left cord (between 30 and 31). Turn the disc counterclockwise so that "E" is at the top. This time the cord from the top right (between 8 and 9) will go to the right of the bottom right cord (between 22 and 23) and the cord from the bottom left will go to the left of the top left cord (between 6 and 7).

5 Turn the board counterclockwise again so that now "S" is positioned at the top, and repeat the top right cord down, bottom left cord up action as in the previous steps.

6 Keep repeating these steps and your braid will start to come through the center of the board.

7 Continue until you have the desired length of braid, remembering that when you attach a clasp it will add an extra ¾in. When you have your desired length, take one cord from each side of the board and tie all four together on the top of the braid. Repeat with the remaining four cords and remove the braid from the board (you could add a small amount of hypo cement glue at this point to stop them slipping undone).

8 Carefully cut off the excess cord and place straight into an end cap with some glue already in place (see page 37). Take the other end of the braid, untie and remove the small length of thread and glue this end into an end cap. Leave for a few hours for the glue to set properly.

Tip

If you need to put the board down mid-braid, place a cord so you have 3 cords at the bottom—this way you will always know exactly where you left off.

Using Clam Shell Endings with Natural Silk Thread

Natural silk thread is a lovely thread to work with. It is strong, you can position and secure beads by tying knots on it, and it has a wonderful soft drape. Most natural silk is sold in 2 yard lengths on small cards, and there is normally a little needle woven into the end of the thread to make it easier to string the beads. A popular brand of silk thread is Griffin. In order to attach a clasp to the end of natural silk thread, you will need to use clam shell endings.

1 Begin by unraveling the silk thread from the card. Make a simple overhand knot (see page 88) in the thread at the opposite end to the needle. Slide a clam shell ending onto the needle, with the hinge part uppermost.

2 Push the clam shell ending to the knotted end of the thread, and cut off any excess thread beyond the knot. At this stage you can dab a little hypo cement glue onto the knot for extra security. Close the clam shell ending over the knot with chain nose pliers.

3 Make another overhand knot straight after the clam shell ending. You now have an ending to attach a jump ring and clasp onto (see page 79).

Positioning Knots on Silk Thread

Due to its slippery nature, getting knots into just the right spot on silk thread can prove a little challenging.

1 Pinch the thread with your thumb and index finger where you want the knot to go.

2 Wrap the longer length of thread around your middle finger and grip it with your thumb and index finger as you pull the long length through the loop you have just created.

3 When you have pulled the thread all the way through, you can release the loop from your thumb and index finger, but keep your thumb and index finger on the thread where you want the knot to go.

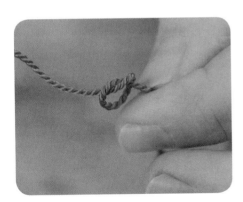

4 With your free hand, carefully pull the longer length of silk away as you push the loop back toward where you want the knot to be.

5 When you have reached the correct position for the knot, pull the thread tight to secure it in place.

Stitching Techniques

Bead Stitching

By threading seed beads together in different ways you can create many textural patterns and interesting effects. The diagrams here show how the thread should be passed from one bead to the next in order to create the desired patterns, so make sure you work in good light so you can see what you are doing.

Ladder Stitch

As well as being a stitch in its own right, ladder stitch is also the base for other stitches such as chenille stitch. It is a good stitch to learn if you are a beginner, as it is quick to stitch and is comprised of only one row. The threads go through each bead a few times which makes jewelry made with ladder stitch fairly durable.

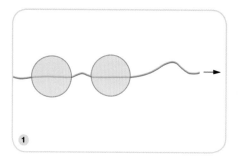

1 Thread a beading needle with a comfortable length of beading thread (arm's length is usually a good choice). Pick up two beads and position them toward the end of the thread, leaving at least a 3in tail.

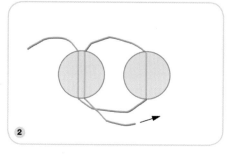

2 Pass the needle through the first bead one more time to form a circle with the thread. As you pull the thread through the bead, both beads will realign so that they sit side by side rather than end to end.

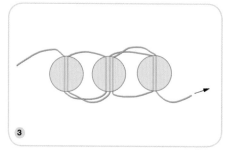

3 Pass the thread up through the second bead and pick up a third bead. Pass the needle up through the second bead once more and down through the third bead a second time.

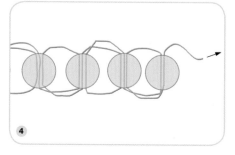

4 Continue adding beads in this way until you have the desired length of ladder stitched beads.

Tip
You can experiment with using two or three beads at each stitch. Treat the beads for each "rung" of the ladder as if they were one bead.

Chenille Stitch Bracelet page 190

Tubular Ladder Stitch

This is useful when you need to create a solid tubular
base for a less stable tubular stitch such as chenille stitch.

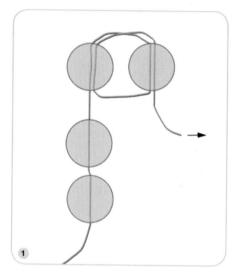

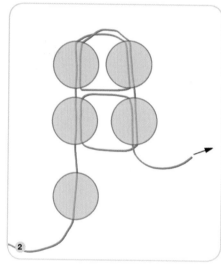

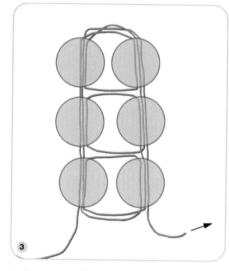

1 Thread on the number of beads you want in
your columns, for example if you would like
each ladder stitch column to be three beads
high, thread on three beads. Holding the tail
thread and the first two beads you threaded
in one hand, pick up a fourth bead, bring
the needle round and up through bead 3
a second time, and back down bead 4.
This creates a ladder stitch between beads
3 and 4.

2 Pick up a fifth bead, and take the needle
up through bead 2, then back down
bead 5, creating another ladder stitch.

3 Pick up a sixth bead, take the needle up
through bead 1 and back down through
bead 6. This creates the third ladder stitch,
and should give you two columns and three
rows of ladder stitch. Take the thread up
beads 1, 2, and 3, then down beads 4, 5,
and 6 to secure all the beads in place.

4 You are now ready to add more beads to
each of the three rows, building additional
columns. Depending on the size of the
beads and how big you want your tube to
be will determine how many columns you
wish to add, but as a guide 6–8 will create
a good tube shape. Turn the section so that
the working thread is at the bottom.

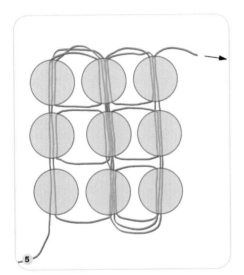

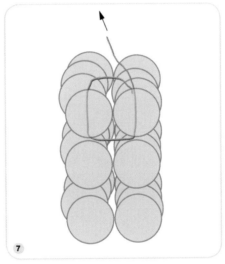

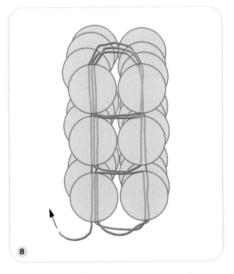

5 Pick up a seventh bead and take the thread down through bead 6 and back up through bead 7. Add an eighth and ninth bead in the same way, then bring the needle down through beads 4, 5, and 6, and up through beads 7, 8, and 9 to secure the third column.

6 Turn the piece so that the working thread is at the bottom, and add the fourth column by adding beads 10, 11, and 12 in the same way that you added beads 7, 8, and 9. Bring the needle all the way down column 3 and up column 4 before beginning the next column. Continue in this way until you have the desired number of columns. Remember to keep the thread tight at all times so that the beads stay in place.

7 When you have added enough columns to make a tube, bend the piece in half. Hold the two end columns together so the working thread is coming out the top of the piece on the right-hand side. Take the thread down through the top bead on the left-hand side and then back up through the top bead on the right-hand side.

8 Take the needle down two beads on the left-hand side, and then back up through the center bead on the right-hand side. Then take the needle down the center and bottom bead on the left-hand side, and back up the bottom bead on the right-hand side, and down the bottom bead on the left, ladder stitching the two end columns together. Secure by bringing the needle up all three beads on the right and down all three beads on the left. You now have a base to continue with another stitch.

Peyote Stitch

This stitch creates a flat beaded "fabric" that drapes beautifully yet has enough strength to form jewelry that will last for years. It can be worked as even-count or odd-count, depending on whether there are an even or odd number of beads in each row, and can also be used to create beaded tubes. The technique shown here is for even-count flat peyote stitch.

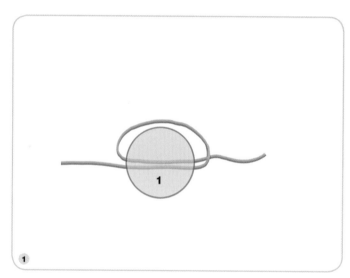

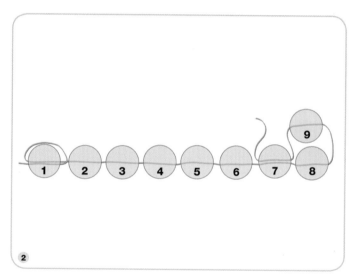

1 Thread a beading needle with beading thread, and thread on one bead to act as the stop bead. Position this bead 12in from the end of the thread, and bring the needle round and back up through the bead, pulling the thread so the bead is secured in place.

2 Now thread on an odd number of beads to create the desired width for each row. With the stop bead included in the count you will have an even number of beads on your thread. In this example we are using eight beads in total. Pick up a ninth bead and bring the needle back through bead 7 (skipping bead 8 at the end of the first row). As you pull the thread tight, bead 9 should sit on top of bead 8.

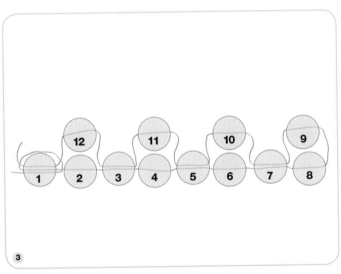

3

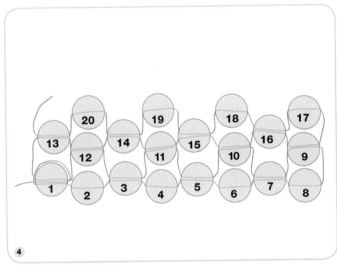

4

3 Pick up a tenth bead, skip bead 6, and bring the needle back through bead 5. Continue in this way until you reach the end of the row, finishing by coming back through bead 1.

4 Continue adding beads in this way, filling in the gaps between beads, then working back in the other direction once you reach the end of a row. Always make sure the thread is pulled tight to keep the tension and this will also help to keep the beads positioned correctly. Note that the way rows are counted in peyote stitch is diagonally, so in the illustration above there are four completed rows.

5 Once you have stitched the length of peyote stitch you need, take the thread all the way back through the last eight beads you threaded for additional security, and then around and back through the final bead like you did with the first stop bead.

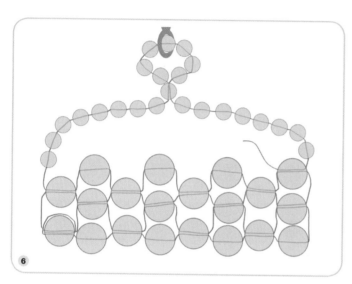

6

6 To attach a clasp, go back to the end you started with, and pull the thread from the stop bead. Thread a beading needle onto the tail thread and pick up 15 15/0 seed beads and one half of a toggle clasp. The toggle clasp needs to have a large enough attachment loop to pass over the seed beads you have just added. With nine beads positioned on your thread down toward your bracelet, bring the needle back through bead 9 and pull it tight. This should secure the toggle clasp within a beaded loop of thread. Pick up 8 more beads and come through the top bead on your bracelet on the opposite side. Now when you pull it all tight your clasp should fit into place.

7 Bring the needle back through the first bead on the top row, and add another bead to fill in the gap. Repeat all along the row to give a more even finish to the piece. Bring the needle through the last two beads at the end of the row, and then through all of the beads added to attach the clasp to give some additional strength.

8 Bring the needle back through the beads on the final row, including the "filler" beads you added. Once you have done this, tie the thread off by coming up in between two beads that are side by side, making a loop with the thread and bringing the end through. Pull tightly, and repeat in the same place. Bring the needle through a few more beads and repeat the knotting action. Bring the needle through the beads to the edge of the piece, bring it down a few rows and repeat the knotting action between beads along the edge a couple of times. Take the thread through the beads to the center of the piece and cut it close to the beads. Repeat at the other end of the clasp.

Tip
You need to take into account the extra length that the clasp will add to your bracelet, when you are creating your piece.

Changing Thread on Peyote Stitch

When carrying out any bead stitching projects you will usually need to change thread mid-project, as it is difficult to work with very long lengths of thread. For flat peyote stitch, you'll need to weave the new thread from the side it is needed to the opposite side and back again, anchoring the thread with knots as you go. You should have the new thread in the same position that the old thread ended.

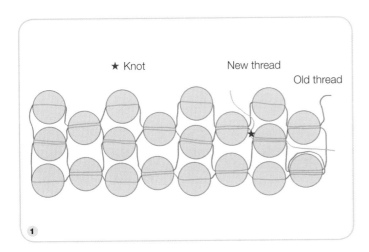

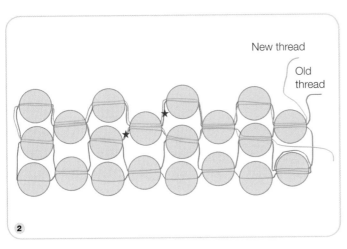

1 When you begin to run out of thread, stop at the end of a row, leaving at least a 6in tail. Thread another needle with a new length of thread (2 yards is a good length to work with). Insert the needle one bead in from the edge, two or three rows down from the latest row. Pull the needle through the bead, leaving a short tail on the other side, and tie an overhand knot (see page 88) around the base thread that runs between the beads. Pull firmly to secure the new thread.

2 Bring the new thread through the relevant beads to the opposite side, following the original thread path and tying another overhand knot halfway across to anchor it between the beads. Move one row up and weave the thread, following the original path to the opposite side, tying a knot halfway across the row, and exiting the last bead you added, in line with the old thread.

3 You now need to secure and hide the thread ends within the piece. Take the needle attached to the old thread and push it through the bead directly below it. Tie an overhand knot around the base thread that runs between the beads, insert the needle through a few more beads, following the path of the weave, and tie another knot around the base threads. Continue to the other side of the piece, then take the thread back to the middle of the project on the next row down, knotting it to the base thread after every few beads. Once you reach a central position, tie a double overhand knot (see page 89) around the base thread, and pull this knot back into the beads by taking the thread through a couple more beads. Trim the thread close to the beads.

4 Thread the needle onto the new tail thread and in the same way that you secured the end of the old thread, secure the thread within the piece and trim the excess close to the beads.

Chenille Stitch

This is a lacy effect tubular stitch that should always begin on top of a tubular ladder stitch foundation consisting of eight three-bead columns (see page 102). It is best to learn chenille stitch using 8/0 seed beads in two colors—a background color and a contrast color.

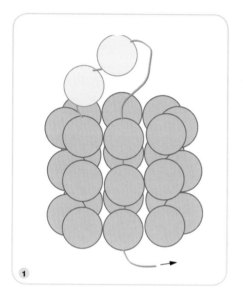

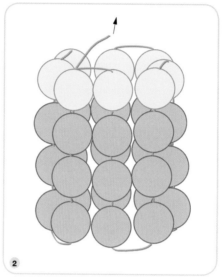

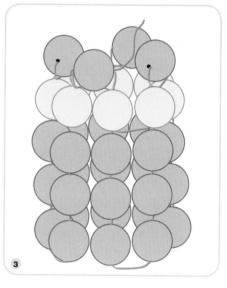

1 Create a tubular ladder stitch base of eight three-bead columns with size 8/0 seed beads (see page 102). Pick up two seed beads in your background color and take the thread all the way down the next column of ladder stitch.

2 Go up through the next ladder stitch column, pick up another two seed beads in the background color, go down the next ladder stitch column, and then up the next column. Continue in this way until you have gone all the way around the base, and when you come up the last column of ladder stitch bring the needle through the first background color seed bead that you added. This is called stepping up.

3 Now pick up one seed bead in a contrasting color and go down through the next background bead, up the next background bead, pick up a contrasting color bead and go down through the next background bead, and then up through the next background bead. Repeat all the way around, adding four contrast beads in total. When you have added your last contrast bead bring the needle up through the first contrast bead as well (stepping up). You have now created you first set of chenille stitch.

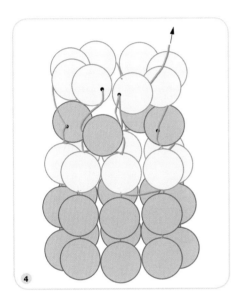

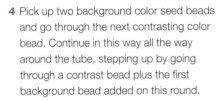

4 Pick up two background color seed beads and go through the next contrasting color bead. Continue in this way all the way around the tube, stepping up by going through a contrast bead plus the first background bead added on this round.

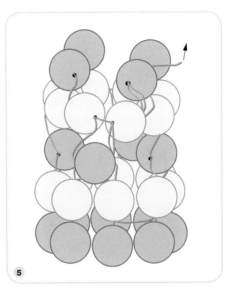

5 Now pick up a contrasting bead and take the thread through the next background bead, skip over the contrasting bead from the previous row, and bring the needle through the next background bead. Continue adding contrasting beads all the way around, and then step up through a contrasting bead.

6 Repeat steps 4 and 5 until you have the desired length of chenille stitch. Ensure you keep the thread pulled tight as you work to hold the beads in the correct position.

Changing Thread on Chenille Stitch

To change the thread when using chenille stitch, you will want to be on a round where the stitch is closed, i.e you have been adding two beads in between beads that were sticking up from the previous round.

1 Take the thread through the beads all the way around the top of the piece once. Remove the needle and thread it onto a new length of thread (2 yards is a good length to work with). Insert the needle into the bead directly in front of where the tail of your old thread comes out, and pull through leaving an 8in tail.

2 Holding the two tail threads continue working chenille stitch as per the pattern. When you have completed another two rounds, tie the loose ends together with a double overhand knot (see page 89). Take the needle, and thread on one of the loose ends. Take it back through a couple of beads, so that the knot sits inside one of the beads.

3 Pull the needle through the center of the tube, between the beads, and cut the thread close to the beads. The end will fall back inside the tube. Repeat with the other loose thread.

Project Gallery

Project Gallery

The projects are arranged in chapters according to their difficulty level, but here you can see the designs grouped by type, making it easier for you to choose which ring, necklace, bracelet, or pair of earrings to make first.

Difficulty levels: Simple * Intermediate ** Advanced ***

Rings

154 Wire Ring *

170 Wire Wrap Ring **

206 Statement Ring ***

Hairband

178 Flower Hairband ***

Earrings

118 **Natural Turquiose and Silver Earrings** ✶

122 **Firework Earrings** ✶

134 **Stacked Crystal Earrings** ✶

154 **Sparkle Butterfly Earrings** ✶✶

174 **Wrapped Briolette Earrings** ✶✶

166 **Tassel Earrings** ✶✶

186 **Chandelier Earrings** ✶✶✶

204 **Beaded Wire-wrapped Earrings** ✶✶✶

Project Gallery

Bracelets

124 Flat Memory Wire Bracelet ∗

136 Weaver Bracelet ∗

142 Wraparound Tubing Bracelet ∗

146 Crystal Macramé Bracelet ∗∗

158 Peyote Stitch Bracelet ∗∗

162 Rainbow Cuff ∗∗

196 Kumihimo Beaded Bracelet ∗∗∗

164 Silver Link Bracelet ∗∗

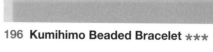

190 Chenille Stitch Bracelet ∗∗∗

Necklaces

120 Beaded Leather Necklace ✶

128 Multicolored Crystal and Silk Necklace ✶

132 Opalite Crystal Teardrop Choker ✶

150 Three-strand Floating Necklace ✶✶

156 Layered Bead Necklace ✶✶

182 Beaded Wire Pendant ✶✶✶

212 Soutache Pendant ✶✶✶

200 Multi Crystal Drop Necklace ✶✶✶

210 Winter Leaf Necklace ✶✶✶

Simple Projects

Natural Turquoise and Silver Earrings

Turquoise semi-precious beads take center stage in this simple earring design. By choosing two special beads it is possible to make a stylish pair of earrings with very few materials and very little time.

Materials
- 2 x 10mm natural turquoise beads
- 2 sterling silver round headpins
- 1 pair sterling silver ear wires

Tools
- Round nose pliers
- Nippers
- Chain nose pliers

Techniques
- Simple loop
- Attaching an ear wire

Time to make
10 minutes

Instructions

1 Slide one of the turquoise beads onto a headpin, and push the straight end of the headpin over to one side above the bead with your thumb.

2 Using your round nose pliers, grip the headpin wire at the top of the bead, then bring the wire up and around the top of the pliers and back down toward the bead.

3 Release your grip of the round nose pliers and reinsert the lower jaw of the pliers into the half loop you have created. Continue bringing the wire round to complete the loop. Trim back the excess wire with nippers. Use your chain nose pliers to re-align and straighten the loop.

4 Take one of the ear wires, and using your chain nose pliers open up the loop by pulling it toward you slightly.

5 Slide the loop at the top of the bead onto the ear wire and then close up the loop on the ear wire (see page 71). Repeat steps 1–5 to make the second earring to match.

Beaded Leather Necklace

By using a fairly thin leather cord and beads with fairly large holes, it is possible to string beads directly onto leather in this project. Using simple overhand knots holds the beads in the desired positions for the design.

Materials

- 59in brown leather cord, 1.5mm diameter
- 2 brass fold-over cord ends
- 9 silver sparkly metal beads with 2mm hole
- 9 gold sparkly metal beads with 2mm hole
- 9 brass sparkly metal beads with 2mm hole
- 2 x 5mm brass jump rings
- 1 x 14mm brass lobster clasp

Tools

- Chain nose pliers
- Scissors

Techniques

- Using fold-over cord ends
- Overhand knot
- Opening and closing jump rings

Time to make

20 minutes

Instructions

1 Attach a fold-over cord end to one end of the leather cord (see page 80). Give the fold-over cord end a final squeeze with the chain nose pliers to make sure the leather cord is held in place securely.

2 Tie an overhand knot (see page 88) in the leather cord next to the cord end. Thread on a sparkly silver bead and tie another knot so that the bead is held firmly between the knots. Thread on a sparkly gold bead, knot the cord as before, and then add a sparkly brass bead, and knot the cord again. Continue adding beads and knotting the cord in this sequence until you have made a 16in long necklace.

3 When you have finished knotting all of the beads in place, cut any excess leather cord, leaving a ⅝in tail after the final knot.

4 Attach the second cord end to the end of the cord.

5 Once the cord ends are in place, use a jump ring at each end to attach the lobster clasp (see page 79).

Firework Earrings

With some inexpensive materials and a few crystal beads you can make a glamorous pair of earrings. You can adjust the amount of wires you hang from the ear wires if you don't want your earrings to be so big, even just one wire hanging will create a stunning yet simple earring.

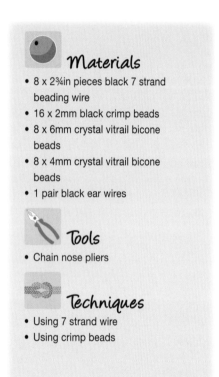

Materials
- 8 x 2¾in pieces black 7 strand beading wire
- 16 x 2mm black crimp beads
- 8 x 6mm crystal vitrail bicone beads
- 8 x 4mm crystal vitrail bicone beads
- 1 pair black ear wires

Tools
- Chain nose pliers

Techniques
- Using 7 strand wire
- Using crimp beads

Time to make
20 minutes

Instructions

1 Take a length of 7 strand wire and make a fold at 1½in. Slide a crimp bead up both ends of the wire to just below the fold, making sure the wires are not crossing over. Flatten the crimp bead with the chain nose pliers (see page 82), and separate the two wires slightly.

2 Thread a 6mm bicone bead onto the shorter wire, place a crimp bead on the very end of the same wire and flatten it with the chain nose pliers so that it stays in place and stops the bicone bead falling off.

3 Thread a 4mm bicone bead onto the longer wire, and fix a crimp bead to the end of the wire as you did in step 2.

4 Repeat steps 1–3 for the remaining seven strands of wire, alternating the type of beads you use on the shorter and longer lengths. You should now have eight strands of folded wire with beads on, four for each earring.

5 Open the loop of the first ear wire with the chain nose pliers. Take a folded wire strand and insert the ear wire loop end into the loop at the top of the folded wire above the crimp bead. Slide another three folded wires onto the ear wire loop, alternating the way they face, and then close the loop of the ear wire with the chain nose pliers. Repeat for the second ear wire, and your earrings are complete.

Flat Memory Wire Bracelet

Beads are attached to flat memory wire by first threading them onto fine wire, and wrapping this around the thicker memory wire. To finish the piece off some charms are added to the ends to give it that extra bit of detail. Flat memory wire is only available in silver or gold but you could experiment with different colored wire for the wrapping.

Materials

- Flat memory wire
- 39½in 26Ga wire
- Approximately 45 mixed 4mm beads
- 6 headpins
- 2 x 5mm jump rings

Tools

- Memory wire cutters
- Round nose pliers
- Nippers

Techniques

- Working with memory wire
- Beaded wire coiling
- Simple loop

Time to make
45 minutes

Instructions

1 Use the memory wire cutters to cut off one and a half wraps of flat memory wire. Bend one end of the wire around the tip of the round nose pliers, creating a loop. If the wire breaks when you bend it, try bending it in the opposite direction.

2 Take the end of the 26Ga wire and hold it against the memory wire, ¼in from the loop. Wrap it around the memory wire toward the loop two or three times; the coils shouldn't touch at this stage.

3 Start making tight coils around the memory wire away from the loop, going back over the loose coils you previously made. Once you have covered the loose coils with tighter coils, you can begin adding your beads. »

4 Thread a bead onto the thinner wire, positioning it onto the memory wire, and then make four tight coils directly after the bead to secure it into place. Continue threading beads on in this way (one bead, four coils) until the beaded part of the memory wire overlaps the looped end by 1¼in. Do not cut the 26Ga wire.

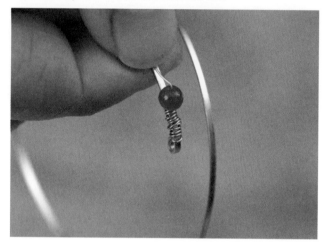

5 Measure ⅝in from the last bead and cut off any excess memory wire. Bend the end of the memory wire around your round nose pliers, creating a loop. Pinch it closed with your chain nose pliers, if necessary.

6 Complete the final few coils with the 26Ga wire toward the loop you have just made, cut off any excess and pinch the end in with your chain nose pliers so that it sits snugly in among the coils.

7 Take the six headpins and place a small bead onto each one. Create a simple loop above each bead (see page 70), snip off excess wire and straighten up the loops with chain nose pliers.

8 Take the first jump ring, open it slightly (see page 79), slide on three beads and then the loop at one end of the bracelet. Close the jump ring. Repeat for the other end of the bracelet.

Multicolored Crystal and Silk Necklace

The bright colors of the crystals really stand out against the black silk thread, creating a simple but eye-catching necklace.

Materials
- 2yd black silk bead cord, size 8, on a card
- 2 black clam shell endings
- 4 x 4mm pink crystal bicone beads
- 2 x 8mm turquoise crystal round beads
- 2 x 8mm topaz crystal round beads
- 2 x 4mm black crystal bicone beads
- 1 x 8mm red crystal round bead
- 2 x 8mm green crystal round beads
- 2 x 4mm red crystal bicone beads
- 1 x 8mm pink crystal round bead
- 2 x 4mm turquoise crystal bicone beads
- 1 x 8mm black crystal round bead
- 2 x 5mm black jump rings
- 1 x 12mm black lobster clasp
- 2in black extension chain

Tools
- Beading needle (optional)
- Chain nose pliers

Techniques
- Positioning knots on silk thread
- Attaching clam shell endings
- Adding a clasp with jump rings

Time to make
20 minutes

Instructions

1 Begin by unwinding the silk thread from its card. It should be pre-threaded onto a needle, but if not, thread one end onto a beading needle. Make a simple overhand knot (see page 88) in the thread at the opposite end to the needle.

2 Slide a clam shell ending onto the thread up to the knot. Trim off any excess thread at the end of the knot and close the clam shell ending over the knot you have just made with chain nose pliers (see page 96).

Tip
You can dab a little hypo cement glue onto the knot before you close your clam shell for extra security.

3 Make another overhand knot in the cord straight after the clam shell ending.

4 Measure 1in along the thread and make another knot (see page 97 for how to position knots on silk thread).

5 Thread on your first set of beads: a 4mm pink bicone bead, an 8mm turquoise round bead, and another 4mm pink bicone bead. Slide them up to the knot and then secure in place with another knot directly after them. »

6 Measure 1in along the thread, make another knot, and then thread on an 8mm topaz round bead, followed by another knot.

7 Measure another 1in along your thread and position a knot. Thread on a 4mm black bicone bead followed by an 8mm red round bead and another 4mm black bicone bead. Then tie a knot to hold these in place.

8 Repeat steps 6 and 7, alternating single beads and clusters of three beads, spaced 1in apart. Work in the following order:
- 8mm green round bead
- 4mm red bicone bead, 8mm pink round bead, 4mm red bicone bead
- 8mm topaz round bead
- 4mm turquoise bicone bead, 8mm black round bead, 4mm turquoise bicone bead
- 8mm green round bead
- 4mm pink bicone bead, 8mm turquoise round bead, 4mm pink bicone bead

9 Measure 1in from the knot after the final set of beads, and make another knot.

10 Slide on a clam shell ending, facing upward this time so that you can tie the final knot into the clam shell.

11 Cut off any excess thread, and then close the clam shell over the final knot with chain nose pliers.

12 Add a 5mm jump ring to each clam shell ending (see page 79), attaching a lobster clasp to one jump ring before closing and an extension chain to the other.

Opalite Crystal Teardrop Choker

This necklace design works well as a choker as the opalite teardrop beads sit perfectly just below the neckline. The turquoise bicone beads provide a contrast that brings out the unusual colors of the opalite.

 ## Materials

- 20in 19 strand beading wire
- 2 x 1.8mm silver crimp tubes
- 1 x 14mm silver lobster clasp
- 2 x 5mm silver crimp covers
- 41 x 4mm turquoise AB crystal bicone beads
- 12 x 8mm opalite teardrop bead
- 1 x 5mm silver closed jump ring

 ## Tools

- Chain nose pliers
- Nippers

 ## Techniques

- Attaching a clasp using crimp tubes and crimp covers

Time to make

20 minutes

Instructions

1 Slide a crimp tube onto the wire and position it 1½in from the end. Thread on a lobster clasp and take the wire back through the crimp tube. Push the crimp tube back up toward the clasp (see page 82).

2 Using your chain nose pliers, flatten the crimp tube so that it holds the wire securely in place.

3 Pull the shorter length of excess wire out to one side, then trim it back as close to the crimp tube as possible with the nippers.

4 Use your chain nose pliers to close the crimp cover over the crimp tube (see page 83).

5 Thread on the bicone and teardrop beads alternately, until your necklace measures 14½in, beginning and ending with a bicone bead.

6 Letting the necklace lie in its natural shape (this prevents too much tension when you finish the necklace), slide on a crimp tube and the closed jump ring. Loop the wire back through the crimp tube, pulling the jump ring back toward the beads but leaving just enough room for the crimp cover to go on.

7 Flatten the crimp with the chain nose pliers. Pull the excess wire out to the side and trim the excess close to the crimp tube as before. Add the crimp cover to finish the necklace.

Stacked Crystal Earrings

Separating two contrasting colors with spacer beads makes the crystal beads stand out even more. This design involves a wrapped loop technique, which gives a more secure and professional finish.

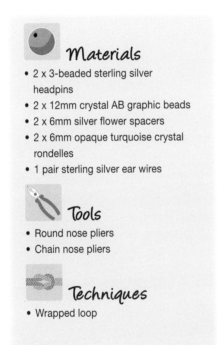

Materials

- 2 x 3-beaded sterling silver headpins
- 2 x 12mm crystal AB graphic beads
- 2 x 6mm silver flower spacers
- 2 x 6mm opaque turquoise crystal rondelles
- 1 pair sterling silver ear wires

Tools

- Round nose pliers
- Chain nose pliers

Techniques

- Wrapped loop

Time to make

15 minutes

Instructions

1 Thread beads onto each headpin in the following order: graphic bead, spacer bead, rondelle bead.

2 Bend each headpin over to one side slightly and make a wrapped loop (see page 72).

3 Grip the wire above the beads with round nose pliers and take the wire up and over the top of the tool, to begin the loop. When you are unable to take the wire around any further, remove the pliers and then reinsert the lower jaw to allow you to continue taking the headpin wire round to complete the loop.

4 Grip the completed loop with chain nose pliers, so that you can get a good hold, and wrap the rest of the wire back down toward the bead stack a few times.

5 Cut off any excess wire and tuck the end in between the coils with chain nose pliers.

6 Attach each bead stack to an ear wire (see page 71).

Weaver Bracelet

This is a great design if you want to have beads all the way around a necklace or bracelet but you don't have enough beads. By using this technique you are able to separate the beads by weaving the beading wire in between them, creating a beautiful effect but using fewer beads.

Materials

- 23½in black 7 strand beading wire
- 2 x 2.5mm crimp tubes
- 1 black toggle clasp
- 2 x 5mm black crimp covers
- 6 purple rock crystal nuggets
- 4 x 8mm pink round hematite beads
- 3 x 6mm clear Australian frosted round beads
- 4 x 3mm multicolored hematite cubes
- 3 x 4mm purple glass pearls

Tools

- Chain nose pliers
- Nippers

Techniques

- Attaching a toggle clasp
- Simple weaving with 7 strand beading wire

Time to make

15 minutes

Instructions

1 Use nippers to cut the beading wire in half to give two separate pieces measuring 11¾in long.

2 Slide a crimp tube onto both strands of wire and then slide on one side of the toggle clasp. Take both wire ends back through the crimp tube, and push the crimp tube up to the clasp. Flatten the crimp tube with chain nose pliers to secure the wire and toggle clasp (see page 82).

3 Take the shorter, excess wires out to one side and cut it with the nippers as close to the crimp tube as you can. Close a crimp cover over the crimp tube (see page 83).

4 The design of this bracelet relies on a random placement of beads, so mix up the five bead types and thread them as they come. Slide the first bead onto one wire, slide the second bead onto both wires, and slide the third bead onto the other wire. Repeat this sequence until you have reached the desired length of your bracelet (see page 67).

5 When you have reached the desired length, slide a crimp tube onto both wires. Slide the remaining half of the toggle clasp onto both wires, and then bring the wires back through the crimp tube. Flatten the tube with chain nose pliers, trim off the excess wires as before, and close the crimp cover over the crimp tube.

Wire Ring

By using a long piece of wire, a feature bead, and just a few tools you are able to create a really eye-catching ring. This type of design works best with large, flat-backed beads.

Materials
- 1 x 18mm crystal silver night twist bead
- 51in gunmetal 26Ga wire

Tools
- Pencil
- Ring mandrel
- Chain nose pliers

Techniques
- Making a ring shank with 26Ga wire

Time to make
30 minutes

Instructions

1 Use a pencil to make a mark on the ring mandrel $\frac{1}{8}$in lower than the actual ring size that you require.

2 Thread the bead onto the wire and position it approximately 8in from one end of the wire. Hold the bead against the ring mandrel, the center of the bead aligning with the pencil mark.

3 Wrap the longer end of the wire around the mandrel and back through the bead three times. Keep the tension tight at all times. »

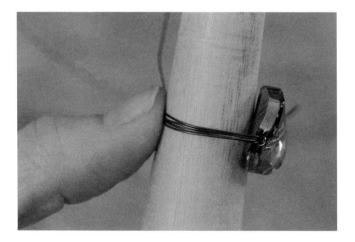

4 Remove the ring from the mandrel, and wrap the shorter length of wire around both sides of the ring two or three times, looping the wire underneath the bead and incorporating the longer length in the wraps to secure it in place.

5 With the end of the shorter wire on the same side as the longer length, wrap the shorter length around that side of the ring two or three times in tight coils. Cut back any excess and tuck the end in with chain nose pliers.

6 Wrap the remaining wire around the ring shank with tight coils, working all the way around the shank (see page 78).

7 Once you have coiled the wire all the way around to the other side, cut any excess off and tuck the end in between the coils with chain nose pliers.

Wraparound Tubing Bracelet

This project shows you how to work with memory wire, a very hard wire made of stainless steel that holds its shape completely. By using the tubing, you do not have to fill the bracelet with beads, making for an economical as well as eye-catching design. Use your favorite colors for the beads and you could even try different colored tubing.

Materials

- 4 wraps extra large bracelet memory wire
- 20in black tubing, 1/8in diameter
- 20 x 4mm crystal bicone beads in assorted colors
- 17 x 8mm crystal round beads in assorted colors
- 2 black headpins

Tools

- Round nose pliers
- Scissors or Nippers
- Ruler

Techniques

- Working with memory wire
- Simple loop

Tip

Do not use your usual nippers to cut memory wire, as it is made of stainless steel and will make dents in them. Always use memory wire cutters.

Time to make

20 minutes

Instructions

1 Using round nose pliers, bend one end of the memory wire around to form a loop. The memory wire is quite hard so you will need to be firm with it (see page 85).

2 Measure and cut a 1in length of tubing. Slide the tubing onto the memory wire, followed by a 4mm bicone bead, an 8mm round bead, and a second 4mm bicone bead. It does not matter which colors you use.

3 Cut and thread on another 1in length of tubing, followed by an 8mm round bead. Continue this pattern of three beads, tubing, one bead, tubing, until you have completed the pattern all the way around the wraps until there is just 5/8in of bare memory wire remaining.

4 Bend the end of the wire around your round nose pliers to create a loop as you did in step 1.

5 Make a charm for each end of the bracelet. Slide a 4mm bicone bead onto a black headpin, bend the wire over to one side and then using your round nose pliers create a simple loop (see page 70). Open the loop a little and attach it to the loop at one end of the bracelet. Close the loop and repeat for the other end of the bracelet.

Intermediate Projects

Crystal Macramé Bracelet

By tying a few simple knots you can create a cute, intricate-looking bracelet. You do not need many tools, and you will learn how to do square, lark's head, and lark's head sennit knots.

Materials

- 3 cards (6yd) white size 4 Griffin silk
- 20mm silver hammered toggle clasp
- 2 large hole silver hammered bead caps
- 4in 28Ga wire
- 20 x 2mm brass heishi beads
- 10 x 7mm opaque green crystal rondelle beads
- 60 x 3mm clear crystal beads
- Hypo cement glue

Tools

- Macramé board and pins
- Thread scissors

Techniques

- Overhand knot
- Square knot
- Lark's head sennit
- Lark's head knot

Time to make

1½ hours

Instructions

1 Unwind all the silk from the three cards and align the thread ends. Thread one half of the toggle clasp onto all three threads and position it halfway along the length. Tie the threads around the clasp with an overhand knot (see page 88) to secure it in place. »

2 Thread a large hole bead cap over all 6 threads and push it up to the clasp. Pin the clasp to the macramé board.

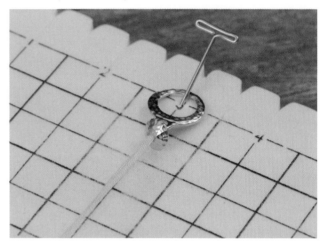

3 Separate the threads into position to begin knotting: choose two without needles at the end to go down the center of the board, take two threads out to the left, and two to the right. Make a square knot (see page 90) close to the bead cap.

4 Taking the two center threads, fold the wire over the threads near the ends and twist the wire ends together a little to hold them together. Pass the wire through a 2mm brass heishi bead, a green rondelle bead, and another 2mm heishi bead, pushing the beads up the wire and onto the threads, then positioning them below the square knots.

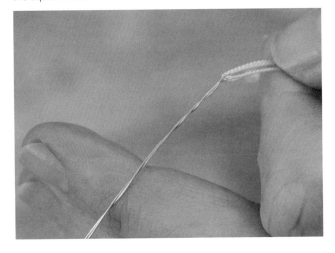

5 You now need to add the 3mm crystals so that they are knotted around this section of beads. Thread a 3mm crystal bead on to one of the threads on the left (the one with a needle attached) and push up to the square knot. Tie a lark's head sennit below the bead (see page 93). Remember that the first loop of a lark's head sennit goes over and under, and the second loop is under, then over. Add two more crystals on the left-hand side in exactly the same way.

6 Repeat step 5 on the right-hand side, adding three 3mm crystal beads securing them in place with lark's head sennit knots.

7 With all six threads tie two square knots (see page 90), making sure that they sit snugly underneath the beads.

8 Continue with this pattern as set in steps 5–7 until the bracelet reaches the desired length. Finish by making two square knots after your final set of beads.

9 Slide a large hole bead cap onto all of the threads, followed by the other half of the toggle clasp.

10 Attach all six threads to the toggle clasp using a lark's head knot (see page 92) and pull tight. Cut back the excess threads close to knot using thread scissors, and apply some hypo cement glue on and around the knot to secure. Slide up the bead cap over the knot to conceal it before the glue dries.

Tip
You may find it easier to knot around your core threads by raising them up with another pin at the bottom of your board.

Three Strand Floating Necklace

This design works well with a simple alternating pattern of beads, and by changing the position of where the pattern starts on the different strands, the groups of beads fall in different places throughout the necklace.

Materials

- 3 x 23½in lengths of silver colored 7 strand beading wire
- 2 x 7mm silver jump rings
- 6 silver crimp tubes
- 6 x 4mm silver crimp covers
- 78 x 2mm silver crimp beads
- 18 x 8mm cream glass pearls
- 42 x 4mm cream glass pearls
- 57 x 3x4mm champagne rondelle beads
- 6 x 5mm silver closed jump rings
- 1 x 12mm silver lobster clasp

Tools

- Bead mat
- Chain nose pliers

Techniques

- Attaching a crimp tube and cover
- Positioning beads using crimp tubes

Time to make

45 minutes

Instructions

1 Lay out the beads for the first strand in the desired pattern on the bead mat. You will need 13 bead stations, arranged as shown. »

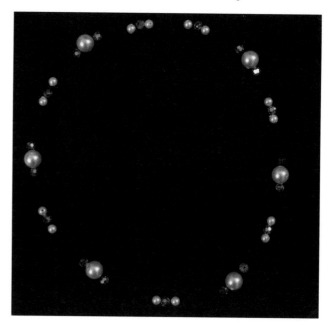

2 Take a piece of 7 strand beading wire and attach a closed jump ring to one end with a crimp tube (see page 82). Cover the crimp tube with a crimp cover (see page 83).

3 Thread on your first group of beads followed by a crimp bead and flatten the crimp bead with chain nose pliers to hold the group of beads in position.

4 Slide on another crimp bead, position it 1in from the previous crimp bead and flatten (see page 84).

5 Continue adding beads in this way, positioning the beads on the wire with crimp beads at 1in intervals, until you have incorporated all of the beads from the design.

6 Attach a 5mm closed jump ring using a crimp tube and 4mm crimp cover next to the final group of beads, and cut off any excess wire. This will be your shortest strand.

7 Repeat steps 1–6 but this time leave a space of $^5/_8$in between the jump ring attachment and the first and last crimp bead at both ends. This will form your middle strand.

8 Repeat steps 1–6 a third time, and this time leave a space of 1in between the jump ring attachment and the first and last crimp bead at both ends. This will form the longest strand.

9 Take the 7mm jump ring and open it a little (see page 79). Thread on the shortest beaded strand using the jump ring at one end, followed by the middle, and then the longest strand. Close up the 7mm jump ring. Repeat at the other end, keeping the strands in the same order and ensuring they are not twisted before you begin adding them to the jump ring. Finally, thread on the lobster clasp before closing up the jump ring.

Sparkle Butterfly Earrings

In this project you need to take care with the direction that you make the loops when you connect everything together, so that each element hangs correctly.

 ## Materials

- 2 crystal AB butterfly beads
- 2 silver headpins
- 2 x 4mm crystal AB bicone beads
- 2 x 6mm crystal AB bicone beads
- 4 silver eyepins
- 2 x 28mm TierraCast teardrop pendants
- 1 pair sterling silver ear wires

 ## Tools

- Round nose pliers
- Chain nose pliers

 ## Techniques

- Simple loop
- Wrapped loop

 ## Time to make
20 minutes

Instructions

1 Thread a butterfly bead onto a headpin, and create a simple loop (see page 70).

2 Thread a 4mm bicone bead onto an eyepin, and make a wrapped loop (see page 72) but before you make the wrap slide the teardrop hanger onto the wire.

3 Open up the eyepin loop underneath the 4mm bicone bead, and slide on the butterfly headpin so that it hangs inside the teardrop hanger.

4 Slide a 6mm bicone bead onto an eyepin and make a wrapped loop, but before you make the wrap slide the teardrop hanger onto the wire.

5 Attach an ear wire to the eyepin loop above the 6mm bicone bead (see page 71). This completes the first earring. Repeat to make a matching pair.

 ### Tip
Make sure that when you are creating the loops for your earring that they go in the right direction, so that everything hangs correctly (see page 73).

Layered Bead Necklace

By using different lengths of beads strung on 7 strand beading wire, you are able to connect the three different lengths straight onto this chain, creating a very elegant necklace.

Materials

- 3 x 12in lengths antique satin brass 7 strand beading wire
- 6 x 5mm closed gold jump rings
- 6 gold crimp tubes
- 6 x 5mm gold crimp covers
- 48 x 5x7mm rondelles in various colors
- 45 x 6mm gold flower spacers
- 2 x 6¼in lengths 10mm gold cable chain
- 1 x 14mm gold-plated lobster clasp

Tools

- Chain nose pliers

Techniques

- Using crimp tubes and crimp covers
- Opening and closing chain links

Time to make

30 minutes

Instructions

1 Take a length of 7 strand beading wire and attach a closed jump ring to one end using a crimp tube (see page 82). Cover the crimp tube with a crimp cover (see page 83).

2 Thread on a rondelle bead followed by a spacer and continue adding alternating rondelle beads and spacers until you have a length of beads from the crimp cover of 3¾in.

3 Lay the beaded wire in a curved shape to replicate how the necklace will lie when worn (so that the tension is correct). Attach a closed jump ring with a crimp tube and crimp cover as you did in step 1, and trim off the excess wire.

4 Repeat steps 1–3 for the second strand of beads, but this time the beading should measure 4½in from the crimp bead cover.

5 Repeat steps 1–3 for the final strand of beads, but this time the beading should measure 5¼in from the crimp bead cover.

6 Take one of the lengths of chain. Open up the link on one end (see page 79) and add the three strands of beads in size order with the longest first. Close the link of the chain.

7 Attach the second length of chain to the other side of the strands of beads as you did for the first, keeping the order the same and ensuring the bead strands are not twisted.

8 Finally, attach the lobster clasp by opening up the end link of one piece of chain, sliding on the clasp, and closing the link. The clasp can clip to one of the links on the other side of the necklace according to the wearer's preferred length.

Peyote Stitch Bracelet

This bracelet is made using even-count peyote stitch. You could experiment by using different types of beads with this technique for different visual effects. It is easiest to learn this stitch with the 3mm cube Toho beads, and if you use two contrasting colors, as here, it is easy to see the pattern as you go.

Materials

- 200 x 3mm turquoise Toho cube beads
- 150 x 3mm baby pink Toho cube beads
- Small selection of 15/0 seed beads
- Toggle clasp
- Black Nymo thread

Tools

- Size 10 beading needle

Techniques

- Even-count peyote stitch
- Attaching a clasp to a flat stitched beaded ending

Time to make

2½ hours

Instructions

1 Thread the beading thread onto the beading needle. Pick up one turquoise bead (the background color) with the needle. Pull it down the thread so that it is approximately 12in from the end.

2 Take the thread back through the bead and pull tight. You have now made this bead into the "stop bead." Add seven more turquoise beads making a total of eight.

3 Now pick up a ninth turquoise bead, and skipping bead 8 take the thread through bead 7 back toward the tail thread (see page 104). Pull the thread tight; bead 9 should be sitting on top of bead 8.

4 Pick up a tenth turquoise bead, skip bead 6 and push the needle back through bead 5. Continue in this way, picking up a bead and threading the needle back through alternate beads on the previous row, until you reach the end of the row. Reposition beads that should be sitting on top of each other as you go.

5 At the beginning of the next row, pick up a turquoise bead and take the thread through the first raised bead from the row below. Keep adding beads in this way all along the row, filling in the gaps between beads on the previous row. Continue working rows of basic peyote stitch in this way until you have completed five rows. »

6 On row 6 begin with a pink bead, go through the next raised bead, then pick up a turquoise bead, go through the next raised bead, and continue picking up alternating pink and turquoise beads until you reach the end of the row.

7 Repeat for rows 7–9, so that you have four rows beginning with a contrast color (pink) bead.

8 Rows 10–13 start with a background color (turquoise) bead, alternating with a contrast bead as you work along the row.

9 Continue beading in this way, working four rows beginning with a contrast color bead and then four rows beginning with a background color bead, until your bracelet is the desired length, taking into account that the clasp will add ¼in.

10 See page 106 for how to attach a clasp to a flat stitch beaded end.

Tip

To count how many rows of peyote stitch you have done, you must count the beads on the diagonal.

Rainbow Cuff

Using memory wire with spacer bars in this project creates a cuff-style bracelet. It will not need a clasp as the memory wire will just clip straight onto the wrist and hold its shape.

Materials

- 5 wraps large bracelet memory wire
- 32 3x4mm purple faceted rondelles
- 32 3x4mm red faceted rondelles
- 32 3x4mm orange faceted rondelles
- 32 3x4mm topaz faceted rondelles
- 32 3x4mm dark green faceted rondelles
- 32 3x4mm light green faceted rondelles
- 32 3x4mm blue faceted rondelles
- 32 3x4mm turquoise faceted rondelles
- 3 four-hole silver spacer bars

Tools

- Memory wire cutters
- Round nose pliers

Techniques

- Using memory wire and spacer bars

Time to make
45 minutes

Instructions

1 Begin by cutting the first piece of memory wire with memory wire cutters. You need one wrap plus 2in, so that the two ends overlap by 2in.

2 Work one end of the cut piece of wire with your round nose pliers to form a loop (see page 85).

3 Thread on the first section of beads. To create a rainbow effect you need to thread the beads on in the following sequence: purple, red, orange, topaz, dark green, light green, dark blue, turquoise.

4 Repeat this sequence a second time and then add a spacer bar.

5 Thread on two more sequences of the rainbow colors and then add a second spacer bar.

6 Thread on a further two sequences of rainbow beads and then add the third spacer bar.

7 Thread on the final two sequences of rainbow beads. Cut any excess memory wire back to leave $^3/_8$in of bare wire. Use the round nose pliers to bend the end into a loop just as you did at the beginning of the bracelet.

8 Repeat steps 1–7 to create a further three bracelets, threading the wire through the relevant spacer bar holes as you work. Ensure you keep the beads in the correct order.

Silver Link Bracelet

This simple design very effectively puts the focus on the central piece. By joining the two lengths of leather together with a square sliding knot, the bracelet becomes adjustable.

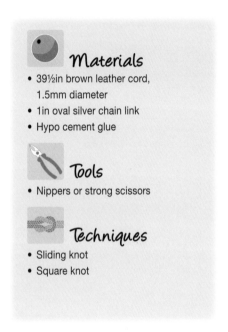

Materials

- 39½in brown leather cord, 1.5mm diameter
- 1in oval silver chain link
- Hypo cement glue

Tools

- Nippers or strong scissors

Techniques

- Sliding knot
- Square knot

Tip

Getting the first knot in place can feel a little awkward but once this is done working with the cord becomes a lot easier.

Time to make

10 minutes

Instructions

1 Cut the leather cord into two 11¾in pieces and one 16in piece.

2 Loop the two shorter lengths of leather through either side of the link chain, creating a lark's head knot (see page 92).

3 Overlap the ends of the two attached cords. Take the 16in length, fold it in half, and make a square knot around the overlapped leather cords (see page 90).

4 Continue making knots in this way until you have completed five square knots.

5 Tie each tail end back toward the sliding knots with an overhand knot (see page 88).

6 Open up the bracelet so that it slides over your hand.

7 Knot the other four cord ends of the bracelet using overhand knots.

8 Cut the ends of the leather right back to the knots and then dab a little glue onto each of the knots. Wait until the glue has completely dried until you move the leather or wear the bracelet.

Tassel Earrings

Tassels never seem to go out of fashion and they are easily incorporated into this earring design.

Materials

- 2yd No.8 khaki natural silk
  (on card with needle)
- 20 x 2mm matt gold hematite beads
- 50 x 1x2mm olivine crystal rondelles
- 8in 20Ga gunmetal wire
- 2 x 10mm brass hammered cones
- 1 pair brass ear wires

Tools

- Thread scissors
- Bead mat
- Nippers
- Chain nose pliers

Techniques

- Knotting silk thread
- Wrapped loop

Time to make
20 minutes

Instructions

1 Unravel the silk thread from its card and tie a knot at the opposite end to the needle. Trim back the thread beyond the knot with the thread scissors, leaving a short ⅛in tail.

2 Using the attached needle, thread on two hematite beads, followed by ten crystal rondelles, followed by another two hematite beads.

3 Measure 3in from the first knot you made and make a second knot on the thread (see page 97). Cut the thread ⅛in from the knot.

4 Put the beaded strand to one side on the bead mat, separating the beads so that half are pushed up against the knot at one end and the other half are pushed up against the knot at the other end, exposing the thread in the center.

5 Repeat steps 2–4 to make four more beaded strands, so that you have five in total.

6 Cut 4in of 20Ga wire with the nippers and bend in half to form an elongated "U" shape.

7 Place all of the threads over the bend in the wire so that the unbeaded center of each thread hangs over the wire.

8 Cross the wires tightly over the top of the threads and twist them firmly together. »

9 Bend the back wire upright so that it is sitting directly above the tassels.

10 Wrap the front wire once around the upright back wire or "stem," to hold everything in place. Cut back any excess wrapping wire (leaving the stem wire long) and pinch the end in with your chain nose pliers.

11 Slide the brass hammered cone onto the wire so that it covers the join between the wire and the threads.

12 Make a wrapped loop above the cone with the stem wire (see page 72). Cut back any excess wire and pinch the end in with the chain nose pliers.

13 Take one of the ear wires and open the loop with the chain nose pliers. Slide on the wrapped loop of the tassel and close the ear wire loop to secure. Repeat all steps for the second earring.

Wire Wrap Ring

In this project you will be shown how to turn a medium-sized bead into a ring. Using minimal materials and tools, you can create an effective and stylish ring from a single bead and a small length of wire. We have used an 8mm round crystal, but you could use any 8mm bead. As you only need one you could use a special one, maybe a semi-precious stone. You can also experiment with different colored wire, as long as it is 20Ga.

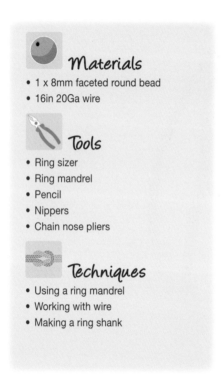

Materials
- 1 x 8mm faceted round bead
- 16in 20Ga wire

Tools
- Ring sizer
- Ring mandrel
- Pencil
- Nippers
- Chain nose pliers

Techniques
- Using a ring mandrel
- Working with wire
- Making a ring shank

Time to make
5 minutes

Instructions

1 Use the ring sizer to work out what size ring you want to make (see page 65). Slide the ring sizer onto the mandrel and make a pencil mark at the bottom of where the ring sizer sits.

2 Slide the bead onto the wire and position it in the center.

3 Holding the bead against the mandrel where you made your pencil mark, wrap the wire either side of the bead around to the back of the mandrel and continue bringing each end all the way round back to the bead. »

4 At this stage the ends of the wire should be parallel, one across the top and one across the bottom of the bead.

5 Hold the ends of the wires, tighten them around the mandrel, then wrap each one once around the bead in the same direction.

6 Keeping the direction the same, wrap one wire at a time half around the bead so each wire aligns with the ring shank. Working in this way keeps the wrapping tight and neat around the bead.

7 Remove your ring from the mandrel. Cut the ends of the wire with nippers to leave 1¼in on each side.

8 Use chain nose pliers to wrap each wire end around and down the ring shank, creating three tight coils to hold everything in place.

9 Cut off any excess wire, ensuring the cut is made on the outer part of the ring shank, otherwise the ring will be uncomfortable to wear.

10 Pinch the cut ends in with chain nose pliers, so that they do not stick out.

Wrapped Briolette Earrings

Wrapped briolettes are a great way to incorporate teardrop-shaped beads into your jewelry designs.

Materials

- 23½in 22Ga wire
- 2 x 20mm rose quartz teardrop-shaped beads
- 2 x 8mm Crystal AB round beads
- 2 x 3in pieces 20Ga wire

Tools

- Nippers
- Chain nose pliers
- Emery paper
- Ring mandrel

Techniques

- Wrapped briolette
- Making your own ear wires
- Making a double ended loop to link beads together

Time to make

15 minutes

Instructions

1 Cut a 10in length of 22Ga wire with the nippers, thread the teardrop-shaped bead onto the wire and position it in the center. Bring the wires up to the top of the teardrop and cross them over each other (see page 74).

2 Bend one wire at the top of the bead with chain nose pliers, so that it sits straight up at the top of the briolette to form a stem.

3 Wrap the second wire around the first and down, covering the wires and the top part of the briolette, keeping the coils tight. Cut any excess wire, and press in the end of the wire with chain nose pliers so that it sits flush against the bead.

4 Slightly bend the wire stem over to one side at the top of the bead, then bend it up and over the round nose pliers to create a loop (see page 72). Wrap this wire around and down the existing wire coil, trim off any excess, and press the end in between the coils with chain nose pliers. Repeat all steps for the second briolette.

5 Cut the remaining 22Ga wire into two 1¾in pieces. Take the first piece and make a loop at one end with the round nose pliers, bending the stem back a little so that it sits at an angle to the loop (see page 76).

6 Thread on the smaller bead, bend the wire over to one side a little directly above the bead, and make another eye loop. Repeat to make another identical piece for the second earring.

7 Attach the teardrop piece to the smaller bead piece by opening the eye loop of the smaller bead, threading on the loop of the teardrop and closing the eye loop (see page 71).

8 To make the ear wires, take a piece of 20Ga wire. Loop one end around the round nose pliers, and then bend the rest of the wire around the small end of the ring mandrel. Cut off any excess wire; rub the ends on emery paper in a figure eight pattern. Slightly bend the end with your round nose pliers and repeat to make the second ear wire.

9 Thread each earring onto an ear wire through the top loop and position within the loop of the ear wire.

Advanced Projects

Flower Hairband

These beaded flowers could easily be incorporated into other styles of hair accessories, for example a barrette or comb.

Materials

- 118½in (3yd 10½in) 26Ga silver wire
- 1056 x 2mm gold seed beads
- 528 x 2mm red seed beads
- 2yd 28Ga silver wire
- 32 x 4mm red bicone beads
- 16 x 4mm gold bicone beads
- Silver tiara hairband, 5mm wide

Tools

- Nippers
- Chain nose pliers

Techniques

- Working with wire and seed beads

Time to make

2 hours

Instructions

1 Cut 39½in of 26Ga wire. Thread on 44 gold seed beads. Position the beads 4in from one end of the wire and bend the beaded part of the wire round to create a loop, twist the ends of the wire together twice to secure the loop. »

2 Thread another 44 beads onto the long wire and make another loop as you did in step 1. Repeat the process two more times until you have four loops or "petals," and arrange them so that they are evenly spaced around the center.

3 Working in the same way as steps 1–2, create a further four petals but position them so that they lie on top of and in between the first four.

4 Repeat step 3 to create a third layer of four petals, positioning them in between those of the previous layer. You should have 12 loops of petals in total.

5 When you have made all 12 petals, wrap the longer length of wire tightly around the center to secure them in place, finishing on the same side of the flower as the shorter "stem" wire. Cut the longer wire so that it is the same length as the stem wire.

6 Twist the two wires together, creating a twisted stem, and put to one side. Repeat steps 1–6 two more times, to make one more gold flower and a red flower.

7 You now need to make four stamens for each flower. Cut four 6in lengths of 28Ga wire. Slide on a red bicone bead to the halfway point of your wire, cross the wires over and twist together either with your fingers or chain nose pliers until you have ¼in of twisted wire.

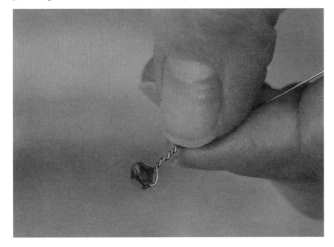

8 Slide another red bicone bead onto one of the wires, bring the wires together and twist again for ¼in from the second bead. Continue in this way, alternating the wire that you slide the red bicone bead onto until you have added four beads. Twist the remaining wires together to the end.

9 Repeat steps 7–8 to make a further seven red-beaded stamens, and four gold-beaded stamens.

10 Take four red stamens and push them down in between the petals at the center of a gold flower, so that the ends come out close to the flower stem. Wrap the ends around the stem to secure.

11 Cut a 4in length of 28Ga wire and bring it around the four stamens just underneath the bottom bicone beads in the center of the flower. Twist the wires together to bring the stamens together. Take the excess wire to the back of the flower and wrap it around the stem.

12 Repeat steps 10–11 for the remaining stamens and flowers, attaching red stamens to the gold flowers and gold stamens to the red flower.

13 The flowers are now ready to attach to the hairband. Wrap each of the wire stems tightly around the hairband to secure each flower. When all three flowers are in place you can put them in their final positions (slightly to one side looks good), and then tighten the wraps of wire by pinching them with chain nose pliers.

Beaded Wire Pendant

Making shapes with wire to create your own pendants is great fun, and
in this design you are shown how to suspend a feature bead in the center.

Materials

- 23½in 20Ga wire
- 1yd 26Ga wire
- 1 x 1¼in rock crystal "feature" bead with hole through top
- 1 strand 1x2mm pale peach crystal rondelles
- 23½in 7 strand beading wire
- 1 x 14mm lobster clasp
- 2 x 2mm silver crimp tubes
- 2 x 5mm crimp tube covers
- 64 x 4mm round electroplated glass beads
- 1 x 7mm closed jump ring

Tools

- Ring mandrel
- Nippers
- Round nose pliers
- Chain nose pliers

Techniques

- Wrapped loops
- Attaching to wrapped loops
- Wire shaping
- Beaded wire coiling
- Crimp beads and crimp bead covers

Time to make
1½ hours

Instructions

1 Cut 11¾in of 20Ga wire. Position the larger end of the ring mandrel in the center of the piece of wire. Holding the center of the wire in position with your thumb, bend the ends around the bottom of the mandrel so that they cross over, creating a teardrop shape.

2 Holding the wires together with your thumb and index finger where they cross over, adjust the size of the teardrop shape so that the large "feature" bead will fit within it.

3 Grab the front wire with round nose pliers at the point where it crosses the back wire. Bend the wire around and underneath the pliers. »

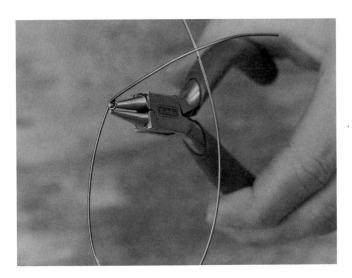

4 When you have made an almost-complete loop, twist the round nose pliers away from you, which should position the small wire loop inside the curve of the teardrop shape.

5 Reposition the wire and hold the ends between your thumb and index finger like before, but this time the wire that extends from the small loop should be at the back.

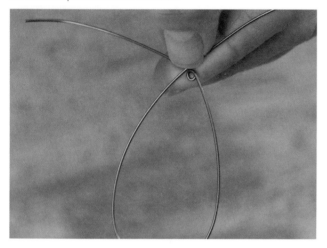

6 Twist the front wire once around the back wire above the small loop, and ensure the back wire extending from the loop is angled to point straight up from the teardrop shape.

7 Leaving the wire that points straight up as it is, cut back any excess from the other wire end and pinch the cut end into the wrapped coil with chain nose pliers.

8 Take the length of 26Ga wire and make a couple of coils around the right-hand side of the teardrop pendant frame with the wire. Take the wire once around the pendant "neck" and to the left hand side, pulling the wire tightly as you work. Pinch the end in with chain nose pliers before continuing.

9 Make two tight coils with the wire on the left-hand side of the pendant, then thread on a crystal rondelle bead, positioning it against the coil (see page 78).

10 Holding the bead in place on the pendant, make two more tight coils directly after it. Continue in this way, adding crystal rondelle beads to the wire and making two tight coils between them until you have gone all the way around the teardrop pendant. The beads should sit on the outer edge of the pendant.

11 Wrap the remaining wire around the neck and stem of the pendant a few times to secure it and cut off the excess at the back, pinching the end in with chain nose pliers.

12 Create a wrapped loop with front-to-back orientation (see page 72) with the stem of the pendant.

13 To prepare the feature bead so it may be attached to the pendant, cut an 11¾in length of 20Ga wire, and slide on the rock crystal, positioning it approximately 3in from one end. Bring the wires either side of the rock crystal up to the top so that they cross over, the longer length at the front. Twist the wires together so that the shorter length sits upright, directly above the top center of the bead, and the longer length wraps around it and comes back down the side of the bead.

14 Wrap the longer wire around and back up the bead toward the top stem, leaving gaps between the coils. Wrap the wire around the stem, cut off any excess, and pinch in the end with chain nose pliers.

15 Begin making a wrapped loop with the stem wire above the feature bead, but thread it through the small loop at the top of the pendant before making the wraps. Complete the wraps to secure the feature bead to the teardrop pendant.

16 Take the 7 strand beading wire and attach a lobster clasp to one end using a crimp bead and crimp cover (see page 82).

17 Begin threading on the 4mm round electroplated glass beads and pale peach crystal rondelles in an alternating pattern and continue until the beading wire measures 8¼in from the clasp.

18 Thread on the pendant and then continue threading beads onto the wire until the beading wire measures 8¼in from the pendant. Finish the necklace by attaching a closed 7mm jump ring close to the final bead with a crimp bead and crimp cover.

Chandelier Earrings

By using wire to create an interesting shape, and loops to attach other beads, this pair of earrings becomes quite elaborate in design. You could make even more impact by decorating them exclusively in very high lead content crystal beads such as Swarovski crystals.

Materials

- 40in 18Ga wire
- 3yd 26Ga wire
- 28 x 4mm AB crystal round beads
- 2 x 18mm AB crystal briolette beads
- 4 x 12mm AB crystal briolette beads
- 1 pair ear wires

Tools

- Nippers
- Round nose pliers
- Chain nose pliers
- Ring mandrel

Techniques

- Wrapped loop
- Beaded wire coiling
- Wire bails

Time to make

45 minutes

Instructions

1 Cut a 20in length of the 18Ga wire, and hold the wire in the center with round nose pliers. Bend the wire ends in opposite directions to create a loop around the round nose pliers. Remove the pliers and grip the loop with chain nose pliers and twist where the wires cross.

2 Make a second loop approximately ³⁄₈in from the center loop made in the previous step, ensuring the loop twists in the same direction, and allowing a little extra wire to be taken up by the twist. Repeat at the other side of the center loop, again twisting the loop in the same direction as the previous two. »

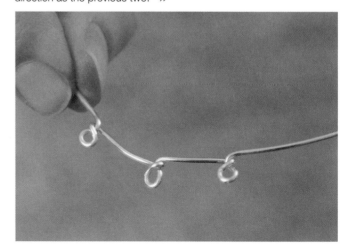

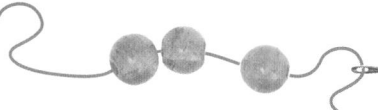

3 Using the thickest part of the ring mandrel, wrap the looped wire around to make a large loop. Bend the wire into the desired teardrop shape by hand and twist the wire ends together so they lock in place. Wrap one end of the wire twice around the other.

4 Cut off the excess wrapping wire and pinch the end in with chain nose pliers. With the remaining end of the wire create a wrapped loop (see page 72).

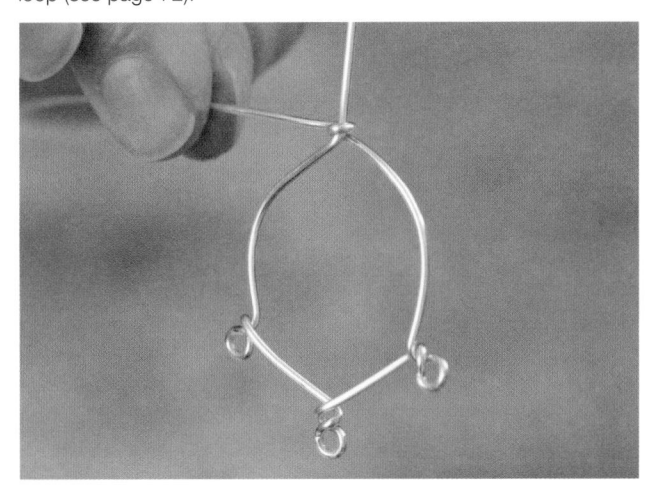

5 The earring frame is now ready for beaded wire coiling (see page 78), using 30in of the 26Ga wire and 14 4mm crystal round beads. Work around the whole earring frame so that it is beaded all the way around the outer edge.

6 Cut a 6in piece of 26Ga wire, slide on an 18mm briolette bead to the halfway point, and then cross the two wires over at the top of the bead. Wrap one wire around the other a couple of times, making sure the wire being enclosed by wrapping is sitting upright from the top of the bead, creating a stem.

7 Cut off any excess wrapping wire and pinch in the end with chain nose pliers. Begin making a wrapped loop with the stem wire, but thread it through the center loop in the earring frame before making the wraps. Complete the wraps to secure the briolette bead onto the earring frame.

8 Repeat steps 6–7 twice more to attach 12mm briolette beads to the other bottom loops on the earring frame. When you have completed all three, attach an ear wire to the frame (see page 71) and repeat all steps to make a matching earring.

Chenille Stitch Bracelet

I have used two contrasting colors of seed beads in this bracelet, making it easier to learn this pretty stitch.

Materials

- ½oz pink size 8/0 seed beads
- 2 x 4mm purple round beads
- 2 silver headpins
- Reel of beige Nymo thread
- ½oz gray size 8/0 seed beads
- 48 lilac size 15/0 seed beads
- 1 x 5mm sterling silver jump ring
- 1 x 14mm sterling silver lobster clasp
- 1 x 7mm sterling silver closed jump ring

Tools

- Size 10 beading needle
- Nippers or thread scissors

Techniques

- Tubular ladder stitch
- Chenille stitch

Time to make

2½ hours

Instructions

1 Prepare the clasp attachment. Slide a size 8 pink seed bead, a 4mm bead, and second size 8 pink seed bead onto a headpin. Make a simple loop (see page 70), cut off any excess wire, and put to one side. Repeat to make a second piece.

2 Thread the beading needle with a length of Nymo thread (about 1 yard works well). Using gray seed beads, complete three rows of tubular ladder stitch with 8 beads in each row (see page 102). This is the foundation of the chenille stitch.

3 Pick up two pink seed beads and take the thread all the way down the next column of the ladder stitch beads.   »

4 Go up through the next column of ladder stitch beads and pick up another two pink seed beads. Bring the needle down the next column of ladder stitch beads and then up the next one. Continue in this way around the tube, until the needle comes up through the first pink seed bead that you added (see page 108). This stage is called stepping up.

5 Pick up a gray seed bead and go down through the second pink seed bead that you added, and then up through the next pink bead. Pick up another gray seed bead and go down through the next pink seed bead, then up through the next and pick up another gray seed bead. Continue in this way until the needle comes up through the first gray seed bead of the round as well as the pink (stepping up). Continue adding rows of chenille stitch (see page 108) until the bracelet measures approximately 6in, finishing on a pink row.

6 The end needs to be finished with ladder stitch. Pick up two gray beads and take the needle down through the pink bead from the previous row.

7 Bring the needle up through the next pink bead, skipping over the gray one.

8 Pick up two more gray beads for the ladder stitch and take the needle down through the next pink bead. Continue in this way until you have gone all the way around, and then step up into the first ladder stitch bead.

9 You now need to connect together all the loose gray beads from the previous round in ladder stitch (see page 100). First go down into the next bead and up again into the first bead, working in the opposite direction. Next go down the second and up the third ladder stitch bead. Then go back down in the second ladder stitch bead and up through the third bead. Continue in this way, joining the beads together in ladder stitch, until you have worked all the way around, picking up the first bead and going down through the eighth.

10 Go up through the first bead of the previous round, pick up two more gray beads, and go down into the second bead. Come up through the next bead, pick up two gray beads, and go down into the next bead. Continue in this way all the way around.

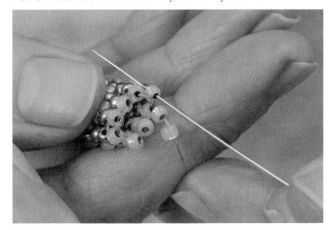

11 When you have gone all the way around, step up two beads and connect these beads together using ladder stitch as you did in steps 8–9. Add one further row of ladder stitch in this way so you have 3 rows all connected together.

12 Now take the thread down three, up the next three, down the next three, and continue in this way until you have gone all the way around the ladder stitch end of the bracelet.

13 Pick up five of the 15/0 lilac seeds beads with your needle, go down all three beads in the next column of ladder stitch, and go up the next three. »

14 Pick up another 5 of the 15/0 seed beads and go down the next column of three ladder stitch beads and up the next three. Continue in this way until you have worked all the way around, threading the needle through the first three 15/0 seed beads you added to complete the round.

15 You will have four loops of five 15/0 beads at the end of your bracelet. The third bead of each loop is the middle bead, and the next stage is to connect these together. Pick up another 15/0 seed bead and push the needle through the middle bead of the next loop. Pick up another 15/0 seed bead and push the needle through the middle bead of the next loop. Continue in this way around the bracelet, and on the final loop go into the bead just before the middle one as well.

16 Take the beaded headpin clasp attachment made in step 1 and place it just inside the top ring of 15/0 seed beads, with the wire loop protruding from the end. Pull the thread tight, closing the ring of 15/0 seed beads around the size 8/0 seed bead on the headpin. Take the thread through the 15/0 beads around the headpin three times, or until the headpin feels secure within the bracelet.

17 Once the headpin is secure, push the needle down two 15/0 and a column of three ladder stitch beads, up the next ladder stitch column and two 15/0 beads, and into the top 15/0 bead. Bring the needle down through the next two 15/0 and column of three ladder stitch beads. Cut the thread close to the beads.

18 Repeat steps 13–17 to finish the other end of the bracelet, securing the thread before you begin (see page 100).

19 Attach a 5mm jump ring and a sterling silver clasp to one end of the bracelet (see page 79). Attach a 7mm jump ring to the other end of the bracelet.

Kumihimo Beaded Bracelet

Kumihimo braiding is both fun and easy. With the use of bobbins you can add beads into your designs for a great effect.

Materials

- 5yd 0.8mm black waxed cotton
- 280 mixed brightly colored 6/0 seed beads
- 6x7mm bell closer with extension chain

Tools

- Round kumihimo board
- 8 kumihimo bobbins
- Thread scissors
- E6000 glue

Techniques

- Kumihimo braiding
- Threading beads into a kumihimo braid

Time to make
1½ hours

Instructions

1 Measure and cut eight 22½in lengths of black waxed cotton. Tie a knot at one end of each piece.

2 For each cord thread on 35 seed beads and tie a knot at the free end.

3 Gather the cords together and push the beads to the bottom of each. Knot the gathered cords all together toward the top end with an overhand knot (see page 88).

4 Push the large knot through the center of the kumihimo board, and while holding it in place with your index and middle finger, position the cords on the board, placing them either side of the N, E, S, and W points (see page 94).

5 Take one of the cords and move the beads away from the very end. Wind the end of the cord around a bobbin a couple of times to secure it, then position 18 of the beads on the cord next to the bobbin and wind them on with the cord. Close off the bobbin, and repeat for the other seven cords.

6 Position the kumihimo board so that it is facing you with N at the top. Work a simple 8 strand braid (see page 94) until you have ³⁄₈in of braided cord protruding from the center of the board. »

7 Once you have approximately ³/₈in of plain braiding, it is time to start adding beads. To do this you braid in the same way as you have been doing, but as you bring the cords over you slide a bead down to the center of the braid, making sure the bead is tucked in underneath the first cord it passes over as you continue braiding.

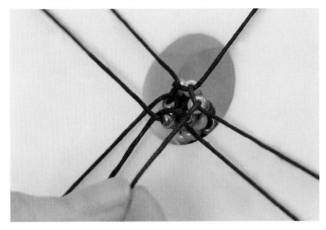

8 Continue braiding with the beads and you will start to see the bracelet taking shape and emerging from the center of the board. Carry on in this way until the bracelet is the desired length, releasing more cord and beads from the bobbins as you work.

9 Continue braiding without beads as you did at the beginning, until the beadless braiding measures approximately ³/₈in.

10 Release one cord from each pair on the board and tie them together with an overhand knot, then repeat for the final four cords.

11 Carefully undo the large knot holding all eight cords together. Take four of the cords and knot them together as you did at the other end of the bracelet, and repeat for the remaining four cords.

12 Cut back the excess cord at each end of the bracelet, trimming next to the knots. Squeeze a little glue into the cord end of one side of the bell closer and firmly push onto one end of the bracelet. Repeat to glue the other side of the bell closer to the other end of the bracelet.

13 Leave the bracelet to dry for at least four hours before you wear it, making sure the glue has dried properly and is holding everything in place.

Tip

If you need to take a break, stop braiding with three cords at the bottom of the board, so you know where the next thread should go when you start again.

Multi Crystal Drop Necklace

This is a delicate necklace made from a variety of beads, grouped together in clusters.

Materials

- 1½yd 26Ga wire
- 6 x 12mm teardrop-shaped green quartz beads (with hole across top)
- 6 x 4mm turquoise crystal bicone beads
- 1 x 20mm teardrop-shaped rose quartz bead (with hole across top)
- 6 gold filled headpins
- 6 x 3mm round crystal pearl beads
- 6 x 3mm brass heishi beads
- 2 x 6mm round labradorite beads
- 1 x 18mm rock crystal nugget center bead
- 2 x 1½in lengths champagne colored fine link chain
- 19 x 4mm jump rings
- 2 x 8in lengths champagne colored fine link chain
- 1 x 14mm lobster clasp
- 2 x 5mm jump rings

Tools

- Bead mat
- Chain nose pliers
- Round nose pliers

Techniques

- Making wire bails

Time to make

1½ hours

Instructions

1 Arrange the beads onto the bead mat according to the design of the necklace in the photograph.

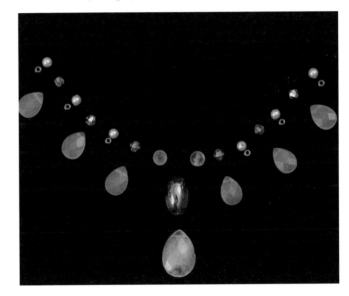

2 With the 26Ga wire, create wire bails (see page 77) for the six 12mm teardrop-shaped beads, the six crystal bicone beads, and the 20mm rose quartz teardrop-shaped bead.

3 Onto each headpin thread a 3mm pearl bead and then a 3mm brass heishi bead. Create a wrapped loop to finish each headpin, trimming off the excess wire (see page 72). »

4 Take the two 6mm round labradorite beads and the 18mm rock crystal nugget, and with 26Ga wire make double end eye loops for each one (see page 76).

5 Connect the 1½in lengths of chain to the central arrangement plus the first 12mm green quartz teardrops and the 20mm rose quartz teardrop using 4mm jump rings, as shown in the photograph.

6 Connect the 8in chains to the 12mm teardrops on either side of the central part of the necklace by opening the jump ring with chain nose pliers, sliding the end link of the chain on, and closing the jump ring.

7 Working on one side of the long chain, count out 8 links up from the central part and attach a beaded headpin with a 4mm jump ring (see page 79). Count another 8 links and attach a teardrop wire bail in the same way. Continue in this way, alternating the teardrop wire bails and beaded headpins until you have attached three of each to one side of the necklace. Repeat on the other side.

8 Attach the clasp to one end of the chain with a 5mm jump ring. Attach the other 5mm jump ring to the other end of the necklace.

Beaded Wire-wrapped Earrings

This design is an extension of the wrapped briolette technique. Tiny crystal beads are used to decorate the wire wraps of the briolette, added with very fine wire.

Materials

- 2 x 12in lengths 22Ga silver wire
- 2 x 16mm flat opalite teardrop beads
- 1yd 26Ga silver wire
- 8 x 2mm purple crystal rondelles
- 1 pair sterling silver ear wires

Tools

- Chain nose pliers
- Round nose pliers
- Nippers

Techniques

- Wrapped briolette

Time to make

15 minutes

Instructions

1 Take a piece of 22Ga wire and thread on a teardrop bead, positioning it in the center.

2 Bring both sides of the wire up to the top of the teardrop so that they cross over. Bend one of the wires back on itself a little so that it rises straight up from the tip of the teardrop. This wire forms the stem.

3 Wrap the other wire around and down the stem, keeping the coils tight, continuing down the upper part of the bead. Trim back any excess wire and tuck the end in with chain nose pliers.

4 To make a loop at the top of the bead, bend the stem over to one side, and then loop it around the lower jaw of the round nose pliers. Wrap the end of the wire around the base of the loop once until it joins the other wraps. Trim off the excess and push the end in with chain nose pliers.

5 Cut the 26Ga wire in half with nippers. Take one of the pieces and attach it to the wrapped bead by wrapping it around the top coils a few times to secure it in place.

6 Thread on a 2mm crystal rondelle, wrap the wire around and down the thicker wire coils, add a second 2mm crystal rondelle, and continue wrapping and adding beads in this way until you have added four crystal rondelles. Finish by wrapping the wire a few times around the neck of the teardrop again, cut off any excess, and tuck the end in with chain nose pliers.

7 Repeat steps 1–6 to create a matching pair. Finally, attach ear wires to each beaded wrapped briolette (see page 71).

Statement Ring

This project shows you how to create a framework for your jewelry designs that can then be decorated in many different ways with beaded wire coiling.

Materials

- 28in 20Ga wire
- 1yd 26Ga wire
- 1 x 6mm electroplated glass round bead
- 8 x 4mm electroplated glass round beads
- 36 x 2x3mm pale peach rondelles

Tools

- Ring mandrel
- Nippers
- Chain nose pliers

Techniques

- Shaping wire
- Beaded wire coil

Time to make

1½ hours

Instructions

1 Mark one size larger than the desired ring size on the ring mandrel. Cut a 20in piece of the 20Ga wire, and wrap it around the mandrel three times where you marked it so that you have two complete loops plus a third almost-complete loop.

2 Take the ring off the mandrel, and wrap each of the ends around the ring shank at "10 o'clock" and "2 o'clock" to hold everything in place, and so that one wire protrudes to the left of the ring and one to the right. »

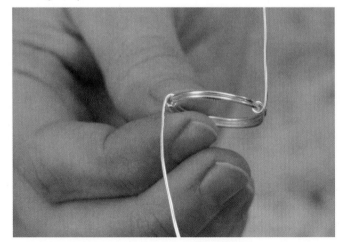

3 Now hold the shank flat onto the mandrel and wrap one end of the wire around the mandrel and back to the shank to create an elongated semicircle. Wrap the wire around the shank a couple of times, in front of the existing wire wraps, to secure the shape. You may find it easier to trim back the ends of the wire at this point to make it easier to pass through the shank. Repeat for the other side. Trim the ends flush with the shank and use chain nose pliers to tidy the wraps and squeeze the cut ends so they tuck in neatly.

4 Take the remaining 8in length of 20Ga wire. You are going to attach this wire to the top of the ring shank, between the wrapped wire loops at "10 o'clock" and "2 o'clock." Hold the center of the wire underneath the ring shank at the top central position and wrap each end up and over the shank to create a loop.

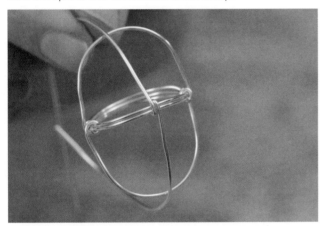

5 Wrap one end of the wire once around the top of the outer oval wire frame of the ring and trim off the excess wire. Wrap the other end of the wire around the bottom of the outer wire frame of the ring to secure it in place and trim off the excess.

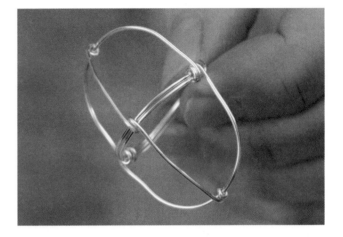

6 The ring frame is complete and ready to decorate. Take the 26Ga wire and attach it to the top center of the ring by wrapping it around the frame a few times. Using the beaded wire coiling technique (see page 78), attach the beads to the ring. Begin by attaching the 6mm glass bead, followed by two of the 4mm glass beads, going down the central wire, adding the 2x3mm rondelles to fill in any exposed wire on the frame.

7 Continue coiling with the 2x3mm rondelles all the way around the edge of the ring frame, until you are back where you started at one end of the central wire. Wrap the wire back up the central wire to the center point of the ring, in between the beads you previously added.

8 Once you have reached the central point, attach two more 4mm glass beads by wire coiling down the left-hand central frame, adding 2x3mm rondelles if needed to fill in any exposed wire, until you reach the outer frame.

9 Work back to the center, wrapping the wire in between the beads, until you reach the central point. Complete the other center wires with beaded wire coiling in this way.

10 When the ring frame has been completely covered with beaded wire coiling, you can cut back the excess wire and pinch the end in with chain nose pliers.

Winter Leaf Necklace

With this necklace it is best to lay out the pieces on a bead mat first, as the design is all about clustering beads and charms together, and decreasing the size of the clusters the further up the necklace you go. In this project I have used silver leaves and electroplated round glass beads, but you could change these for whatever you fancy or have in your bead box.

Materials

- 1 x 25mm silver leaf charm
- 14 x 18mm silver leaf charms
- 9 x 6mm round electroplated glass beads
- 1yd 20Ga non-tarnish silver artistic wire
- 9 x 4mm round electroplated glass bead
- 15 x 4mm sterling silver jump rings
- 9 silver round headpins
- 9 x 10mm sterling silver jump rings
- 2 x 4in lengths 18/14 plain trace sterling silver chain
- 4 x 5mm sterling silver jump rings
- 13mm sterling silver lobster clasp

Tools

- Bead mat
- Round nose pliers
- Chain nose pliers
- Nippers

Techniques

- Double loop connector bead
- Wrapped loop

Time to make
1 hour

Instructions

1 Arrange the beads, charms, and 10mm jump rings on a bead mat in the design of the necklace. There should be a central piece and then four clusters of beads going up each side. »

2 Attach a 4mm jump ring (see page 79) to the large leaf at the bottom center of the necklace.

3 Make a double wrapped loop connector (see page 76) for the 6mm bead that that sits above the large leaf. Repeat this for all of the 6mm beads that fit in between the clusters, so that all nine 6mm beads have double wrapped loop connectors.

4 Place each 4mm round bead onto a headpin, and make wrapped loops (see page 72) on each of them.

5 Connect the large leaf at the bottom to the bead that goes above it with the 4mm jump ring already attached to the leaf in step 2.

6 Attach 4mm jump rings to all of the 18mm leaf charms, and slide on a 4mm round bead before closing each jump ring.

7 Beginning at the center of the necklace, use 10mm jump rings to connect all of the pieces. For the central 10mm jump ring, slide on the large leaf charm and bead piece, the two small leaves and their beads either side of the central piece, and finally the two 6mm connector beads either side of the small leaf charms.

8 Continue linking pieces together up the sides of the necklace with 10mm jump rings. Once all your leaves and beads are connected, add 4in of fine link chain to each side of the necklace, connecting each piece with a 5mm jump ring onto the 10mm jump ring).

9 Finally, add the clasp to one end of the chain with a 5mm jump ring and a jump ring to the other end of the chain.

Soutache Pendant

This pendant is a great design to try when starting out with soutache, which is a type of braiding.

Materials

- Fabric glue
- 1in cabochon
- Small piece beading foundation, slightly larger than cabochon
- Fireline beading thread
- 8in green soutache braid
- 8in beige soutache braid
- 8in cream soutache braid
- 1 x 3mm seed bead
- 15 x 6mm two-hole triangle beads
- 45 Size 11/0 seed beads
- 180 Size 15/0 seed beads
- 2 x 6mm round faceted green AB beads
- Small piece of cardboard
- Small piece soft leather, slightly larger than cabochon
- 17mm gold hammered pinch bail
- 5mm gold jump ring
- 7mm gold jump ring
- 20in gold fine link chain
- 1 x 12mm gold colored lobster casp

Tools

- Size 10 or 12 beading needle
- Scissors

Techniques

- Sewing: backstitch and netting stitch

Time to make

1½ hours

Instructions

1 Use the fabric glue to stick the cabochon to the piece of beading foundation. Let dry.

2 Thread a beading needle with beading thread, make a double knot, go through the beading foundation and stitch the green soutache to the foundation so that it fits tightly around the cabochon, with the free ends located at the top of the cabochon. Ensure you stitch through the groove in the center of the soutache braid.

3 Stitch the cream soutache braid around the green so that it fits snugly up against it and the ends protrude at the top of the soutache, and repeat for the beige soutache.

4 Pinch the soutache pieces together at the top of the cabochon and push the needle through the three pieces on one side. Thread a 3mm seed bead onto the needle and push the needle through the three pieces of braid at the other side, joining all six pieces together at the top with the bead in between. »

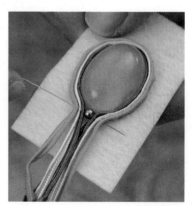

5 Pick up a triangle bead and three size 11/0 seed beads. Push them down the needle and onto the thread, then push the needle through the second hole in the triangle bead and the three braids near the top of the cabochon.

6 Repeat step 5 all around the edge of the cabochon, locating the groups of triangle and seed beads next to each other so that the outer piece of soutache is covered. When you reach the other side of the top of the cabochon, bring the needle back through the central 3mm seed bead, across to the other side, and through the third 11/0 seed bead.

7 Thread on five 15/0 seed beads, push them down the needle and onto the thread, push the needle back through the second 15/0 bead, and thread on a sixth 15/0 bead. Push the needle through the next three 11/0 seed beads, and as you pull the thread through a small loop will form with the 15/0 beads, between the two groups of 11/0 beads. Continue like this, working back around the pendant.

8 When you get back to the other side of the pendant, bring the needle out of the central size 11/0 seed bead closest to the top of the cabochon. Thread on three size 15/0 seed beads and push the needle through the uppermost 15/0 seed bead from the previous round. Thread on another three size 15/0 seed beads and go through the central size 11/0 bead in the next cluster. Repeat all the way around, joining the uppermost 15/0 seed beads from the previous round to the central 11/0 beads from the first round.

9 Bring the needle out through all three pieces of soutache a little above the beaded edging. Thread on a 6mm bead and push down the thread so that it sits snugly against the soutache above the beaded edge. Wrap the three layers of soutache braiding around the bead, and secure them to the back of the pendant with a few stitches.

10 Bring the needle through to the central space at the top of the pendant, thread on a 3mm pearl bead and then push the needle through the layers of soutache to the other side of the pendant. Add another 6mm bead to match the other side of the cabochon and secure the soutache to the back of the pendant in the same way.

11 Trim back the foundation with scissors. Apply glue to the back of the pendant and stick on a small piece of cardboard, cut to shape, to cover up the soutache ends.

12 Cut out a piece of leather to match the shape of the cabochon, and stick it to the cardboard with fabric glue.

13 When the pendant has dried, attach the pinch bail to the central 3mm bead. Use the bail to thread the pendant onto the fine link chain. Use jump rings to attach a lobster clasp to the ends of the chain (see page 79).

Information

Suppliers

Listed below are some of the many manufacturers and suppliers of great quality beads, stringing materials, and findings. Your local bead store will be able to recommend others, as well as offer plenty of help and advice when purchasing products.

Suppliers

Kerrie Berrie
www.kerrieberrie.com

Caravan Beads
www.caravanbeads.net

Bead and Button
www.beadandbuttonshow.com

Holy & Pure Gemstone, Inc.
www.holygemstone.com

Knot Just Beads
www.knotjustbeads.com

Ocean Dreams
www.oceandreamsusa.com

Fire Mountain Gems
www.firemountaingems.com

Fusion Beads
www.fusionbeads.com

Shipwreck Beads
www.shipwreckbeads.com

Unicorne Beads
www.unicornebeads.com

Trinkets by T
www.trinketsbyt.com

York Beads
www.yorkbeads.com

Chicken and the Egg
www.chicken-egg.com

Bead Biz
www.beadbiz.org

Bead My Love
www.beadmylove.com

Beads by Blanche
www.beadsbyblanche.com

Jo-Ann
www.joann.com

Hobby Lobby
www.hobbylobby.com

AC Moore
www.acmoore.com

Michaels
www.michaels.com

Manufacturers

Beadalon
www.beadalon.com
Wire, strand, and cable for bead stringing, jewelry making, and crafts. A reputation for innovative and quality products.

Artistic Wire
www.artisticwire.com
Leading supplier of high-quality craft wire. Offering an extensive line of soft permanently colored copper wire.

Griffin Bead Stringing Supplies and Accessories
www.griffin-store.com
Leading manufacturer of silk thread and high-quality, extremely strong high-tech fibers as well as fine-spun and refined metal wires.

TierraCast
www.tierracast.com
Affordable, quality components that complement a wide range of jewelry and beadwork.

Glossary

Bails Used to turn beads into pendants.

Bead caps Convex metal findings placed either side of a bead to create a more decorative effect by framing the bead.

Bead design board Has multiple grooves molded into the plastic board, with a flocked surface to keep beads in place. They are also marked with measurements so that you can see how many beads you need for a particular piece of jewelry.

Bead mat Provides a flocked surface that is essential for laying beads out on when planning a design as it stops them rolling away.

Bead reamer Has a fine round, pointed file that allows you to smooth away sharp or rough edges inside beads, or to make a bead hole slightly bigger.

Bead stoppers Little springs available in small and large sizes that clip onto stringing material to stop the beads coming off one end.

Beading needles Long, flexible needles with a small eye, enabling them to fit through the holes in seed beads.

Bugle beads Small beads that are shaped like long, fine tubes.

Calipers Used to measure the size of beads.

Charlottes Faceted seed beads that reflect light well.

Clam shells Used to conceal knots. The cups close around the knot, and have loops so that a jump ring and clasp may be attached. Also called Beadtips or Calottes.

Clasp Device that fastens together or opens up easily, allowing a necklace or bracelet to be taken on and off.

Crimp beads Round metal beads that can easily be flattened with chain nose pliers so they stay in place on beading wire.

Crimp tubes Metal beads in tube shape that can be flattened with chain nose pliers so that they stay in position on beading wire.

Crimp covers Shaped like three quarters of a hollow donut, these are used to hide crimp beads or tubes.

Druzy stones Semi-precious beads with tiny glittery crystals on the surface.

End cones May be used to hide stringing ends, especially where multiple strands come together.

Extension chains Can be attached to necklaces or bracelets, giving the wearer the option to change the length.

Eyepins Pins with a loop at one end that can be opened and closed, allowing you to attach other findings.

Fold-over cord ends Used in particular to secure soft stringing material such as leather and fine chain.

French bullion wire / French coil See Gimp.

Gimp Hollow tube of tightly coiled fine wire, also called French bullion wire or French coil.

Headpins Pins with a shaped end to prevent beads or charms falling off.

Jump rings Strong round or oval wire rings that twist open and closed.

Kumihimo Type of Japanese braiding involving multiple strands of cord and a special board called a Kumihimo board.

Lampwork beads Glass beads made by hand with a flame torch.

Macramé Craft involving different knots to create decorative effects. A macramé board and T-pins are often used with small threads to keep them in place while working.

Memory wire cutters Tool used to cut hard steel such as memory wire.

Nippers Strong, small scissor-like tool used for making clean cuts in tough materials such as beading wire.

Pliers Scissor-like tool used to shape and manipulate metal. The jaws vary depending on function. For different types see page 60.

Polymer clay PVC-based modeling clay that can be hardened in a domestic oven. It can be used to make colorful beads.

Rat tail Common name for nylon satin cord, which is used in Kumihimo braiding as well as other knotting and braiding techniques.

Ring mandrel Tapered wooden pole that allows you to form different sizes of wire ring.

Rocailles Slightly flattened, donut-shaped seed beads.

Seed beads Tiny glass beads, generally under 4mm in size, used mainly for bead stitching, weaving and embroidery.

Spacer bars Flat metal bars with varying numbers of holes in them, allowing you to separate multiple strands in your design.

Spacer beads Usually made from metal, these are small beads used to separate larger beads.

Split rings Similar to jump rings but coiled so that the ends overlap.

Wire guardians Rigid horseshoe-shaped metal findings that protect beading wire.

Index

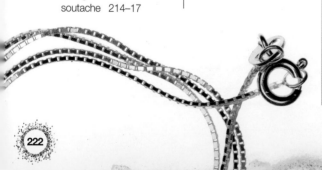

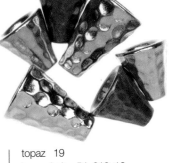

Acknowledgments

I would like to thank Quintet Publishing for giving me this opportunity and Katy Denny for guiding me along the way and for being a great person to work with.

To my sister and best friend, Melanie, for joining me on this creative path of jewelry making and for adding her business mind to make our brand a success.

To Mum and Dad for always supporting and believing in my jewelry designs and helping me to achieve my ambitions.

To Andy for being my calming influence when things got a bit stressful. I love you.

To John and Rita for always offering a helping hand to look after the children, and for making delicious veggie lasagna to keep me going.

To Arabella and Finley for making life more fun.